Using stories

RE and Citizenship

Ages 9-11

Steve Eddy

Hopscotch
A division of MA Education Ltd

Steve Eddy taught English in a comprehensive school in Gloucestershire before entering publishing and becoming a freelance editor and writer. He has published books on Greek, Celtic and Native American myths and beliefs, as well as materials for religious education and guides to English literature. He lives in Wales, where he now teaches part-time in a primary school.

Published by Hopscotch, a division of MA Education, St Jude's Church, Dulwich Road, London, SE24 0PB
www.hopscotchbooks.com
020 7738 5454

© 2005 Hopscotch Educational Publishing
Reprinted 2013 © MA Education Ltd

Written by Steve Eddy
Series design by Blade Communications
Illustrated by Tony Randell
Cover illustration by Pat Murray

Steve Eddy hereby asserts his moral right to be identified as the author of this work in accordance with the Copyright, Designs and Patents Act, 1988.

ISBN 1-904307-98-1

All rights reserved. This book is sold subject to the condition that it shall not, by way of trade or otherwise, be lent, hired out or otherwise circulated without the publisher's prior consent in any form of binding or cover other than that in which it is published and without a similar condition, including this condition, being imposed upon the subsequent purchaser.

No part of this publication may be reproduced, stored in a retrieval system, or transmitted, in any form or by any means, electronic, mechanical, photocopying, recording or otherwise, without the prior permission of the publisher, except where photocopying for educational purposes within the school or other educational establishment that has purchased this book is expressly permitted in the text.

Contents

Introduction		4
1.	**We're all human – Buddhism**	6
	Kisagotami	
2.	**Bad influences – Buddhism**	12
	The King's Elephant	
3.	**Family fairness – Christianity**	19
	The Prodigal Son	
4.	**Loyalty and the law – Christianity**	27
	The Betrayal of Jesus	
5.	**Honesty and fairness – Hinduism**	33
	Lakshmi and the Wise Washerwoman	
6.	**Groups and leaders – Hinduism**	40
	The Monkey King	
7.	**Who makes the rules? – Islam**	46
	Muhammad's Night of Power	
8.	**Respecting beliefs – Islam**	51
	The Cave, the Doves and the Spider	
9.	**Deciding what to do – Jainism**	58
	King Hansa	
10.	**Rights and promises – Judaism**	64
	The Ten Plagues of Egypt	
11.	**Could you be a hero? – Judaism**	74
	David and Goliath	
12.	**Local heroes – Native American**	82
	Monster-Slayer and Born-of-Water Visit their Father	
13.	**Faith and bravery – Sikhism**	87
	The Five Beloved Ones	
14.	**How we treat others – Sikhism**	92
	Gobind Singh and the Donkey	
15.	**Everyone's different – Sufism**	98
	The Shopkeeper and the Parrot	

Introduction

Why citizenship?

In a democratic, multicultural society it is important for children to grow up with a grasp of what it means to be a good citizen, so that they can play a conscious part in making their local and wider community a better place for everyone. In a society like ours, in which political issues are complex and decisions are made by professional politicians, many young people feel that society gives them little and that they owe it nothing. By teaching citizenship at primary level we can help children to understand that they do have an important and rewarding role to play and that they have an effect on everyone with whom they come into contact.

Why religious stories?

A religion is often confused with its outward appearances. It is possible to teach children about rites of passage and the historical origins of religions without them really understanding the philosophy of the religion. The stories of the religions, on the other hand, contain the essence of the religion. Moreover, they show how this essence is played out in a social context.

There are other good reasons for teaching citizenship through religious stories. Stories in themselves are an excellent teaching medium – a fact recognised by many religions. Children identify with the characters and become absorbed in the story. On the simplest level, they want to know what happens next. But when the story is over, there are always questions to ask. All the stories in this book raise questions relating to ethics and citizenship. They encourage children to discuss personal and social issues and to become aware of the choices they have to make as citizens.

The multicultural aspect

Children in our schools come from a wide variety of ethnic and religious backgrounds. Even those from families with no particular religious belief are influenced by their peers and by the largely Judaeo-Christian basis of our society's legal code. The stories in this book are taken from nine different spiritual traditions. They illustrate a wide variety of lifestyles, from all over the world and from different eras. They collectively embody a wisdom whose value is shown by the longevity of the stories and by their shared themes and messages. We live in a society which is hugely diverse, yet our similarities are at least as strong as our differences. The stories will help teach children the universality of human concerns, encouraging tolerance and appreciation of other cultures and ethnic groups.

The structure of the book

Each section is based on a single story. There are two stories for each of the six most widespread spiritual traditions and one story for each of three less well known traditions. Each section begins with teachers' notes. These include:

❏ a short introduction suggesting the number of lessons over which to spread the section and one or two other stories in the book to which it relates;

❏ the main themes of the story;

❏ related Citizenship units;

❏ aims of the lesson;

❏ resources needed (typically, copies of the story and a worksheet);

❏ background: the source of the story and how the story reflects the religion;

- whole class starter: an activity to engage children in the issues raised by the story, particularly those relating to citizenship, before reading the story;

- activities for you to choose from;

- plenary: rounding off the lesson;

- differentiation: ideas;

- extension activities.

How to use the book

We suggest that you do the Starter activity with the class in order to get them thinking about the issues in the story, and relating these issues to their own lives. Then read the story aloud, with the children following it in their copies. You will usually find that the children want to comment on the story and discuss it, so encourage this before settling them down to the activities suggested. You could introduce information from the background section at this point.

Note that a choice of main activities is provided. The easier ones tend to come first, but there are also separate suggestions for differentiation. You could have the whole class working on a single activity, but in many cases it would be possible for groups of children to work on different activities. However, you should all come together for the plenary. After all, citizenship is about a shared experience, and sharing what has been learned is an exercise in citizenship in itself!

The stories

The stories have been retold for this book but their key elements are based closely on original sources. Sometimes different versions of a story are available, in which case the retelling usually merges aspects of these different versions.

The stories take many forms. Some are about the founders of religions or about other significant figures. These are, to a greater or lesser extent, based on historical events but they exemplify features of the religion. For example, both 'The Betrayal of Jesus' and 'The Five Beloved Ones' (the Sikh story of the formation of the Khalsa) are about faith, trust, devotion to a cause, and personal choice. Some feature an historical figure but tell a story that may have been much embellished, invented or taken from elsewhere and ascribed to the historical figure because they embody the teachings.

Some of the stories are intended to teach a specific lesson. For example the Buddhist story 'The King's Elephant' is like an extended fable, teaching that we are morally influenced by the company we keep. The Christian story 'The Prodigal Son' was also told to teach a lesson. At the other end of the scale, the Navajo story 'Monster-Slayer and Born-of-Water Visit their Father' is rooted in the unconscious archetypes of myth. It is not a deliberate attempt to teach a single specific lesson – although it does embody the good citizenship principle of heroic endeavour on behalf of the community. However, you should regard even the more specific stories as jumping-off points for discussion. They are never just an exercise in interpretation.

RE/Citizenship – Ages 9–11

CHAPTER 1

We're all human – Buddhism

TEACHERS' NOTES

This chapter is based on a Buddhist story, 'Kisagotami'. It is about the needs and fears shared by all human beings, and about facing up to the fact that everyone must die. It promotes the idea that recognising our shared humanity is the starting point for a more positive sense of community and communal responsibility. It could be linked to 'David and Goliath' (Chapter 11) and 'The Five Beloved Ones' (Chapter 13), which, in part, are also about facing death. The lesson could be spread over one or two sessions.

Themes
Compassion, shared suffering, death

Citizenship Scheme of Work
Unit 5 – Living in a diverse world

Aims
- To encourage children to appreciate that, however alone we feel, we all share in the 'human situation'.

Resources
- Copies of the story 'Kisagotami' (page 8)
- Copies of the activity sheet 'What we have in common' (page 11)

Background
Buddhism places great emphasis on the universality of suffering, and therefore on the need for us to develop compassion for all living beings, and especially for other human beings. It also teaches that a primary characteristic of life as we know it is impermanence: nothing lasts for ever. Hence, our individual lives are impermanent, but this fact can be a source of fellow feeling and compassion. This is the focus of the story of 'Kisagotami'.

Whole class starter
❏ Display or share out copies of the sheet 'What we have in common'. Lead the children in a brainstorming session about the pictures. What can the children see? What is happening? What issues arise? Some possible answers are:
- We all have to eat and sleep.
- We all are worried or scared sometimes.
- We all want and need to be loved.
- We all want to be liked and appreciated.
- We all make mistakes.
- We all want to feel safe.
- We all die eventually.

❏ Explain that Buddhists believe that because we have all these things in common we should develop compassion towards each other. You could explain compassion as having feeling (passion) for our fellow human beings – and for other living things.

❏ Ask the children to work in pairs and write down responses to the following:
- times when they were very hungry;
- times when they were very tired;
- times when they were worried, scared or felt unsafe;
- times when they particularly wanted to be liked or appreciated;
- the names of people who like them;
- a mistake they have made.

6 RE/Citizenship – Ages 9–11

❏ Now read the story.

Activities

❏ Organise the children into groups of four or five. Ask each group to draw up a two column table. In one column they should list ways in which Kisagotami is unlucky and in the other ways in which she is lucky. Possible points could include: unlucky – she is often ill, her sisters complain about her, she is ill treated by her new family, her son dies; lucky – she is allowed to do the easy jobs, she finds a husband who appreciates her, she has a son and is appreciated as a mother, she is helped by the Buddha.

❏ Next ask the children to discuss and write about two things from each column that they can relate to from personal experience. Help them to see how their own experience relates to Kisagotami's. For example, they won't have had a son die, but they may have lost a family member or a pet, or just lost touch with a friend who moved away or went to a different school. Note: sensitivity is required with this.

❏ Ask the children to work in groups to think what advice they might offer to Kisagotami at different points in her life.

❏ Ask the children to write down what they or the Buddha might say to the sisters and mother-in-law to encourage them to be kinder to Kisagotami.

❏ Ask the children to work in groups to role play key characters in the story: Kisagotami, her father, her sisters, her husband and her mother-in-law. Each could say how they feel at different points in the story.

Differentiation

❏ Give keyword hints to help children fill out the unlucky/lucky table: health, own family, husband's family, son, Buddha.

❏ For advising Kisagotami, suggest the key points in her life: when she lives with her father; when she gets married; when her son dies.

❏ For a more challenging activity, the children could use their ideas for advising Kisagotami and write an 'Agony Aunt/Uncle' letter to her.

Extension

❏ The children could find out about local initiatives aimed at improving the community. They could also try to identify problems in their community and what could be done about them.

Plenary session

❏ Make the point that if we can think of ways to be kinder to Kisagotami, it should also be possible to think of ways to be kinder towards people in general. Ask how we, as children and as adults, could make our community better for everyone. Some suggestions will inevitably be 'don'ts', such as 'Don't throw litter onto the street!' or 'Don't steal!' but it should be possible to find more positive suggestions, such as 'Be polite.' and 'Offer to help if you can see that someone has a problem.'

Kisagotami

"Hey – Kisagotami! Why can't you fetch water from the well? We always have to do your share of the work."

"I'm sorry, sister," I replied guiltily. "I'm doing what I can." My sister's complaint was a familiar one. Although the eldest of my father's daughters, I was the least useful when it came to tackling the hard work that a poor family like ours had to do just to survive. My father used to let me do the lighter jobs. Just now, I was making chapattis, while my sisters fetched water and carried sacks of rice.

"At least that's one thing you can do for a husband," my father sighed.

I knew I was a worry to him. As the eldest daughter, I should be married first – and off my father's hands at last. But no one thought I'd find a husband, because I was so often ill. No one knew what was the matter with me, and my father couldn't afford to pay a doctor.

One day, however, a stranger came to our village. I was at the market when we first saw each other. Luckily it was a day when I wasn't feeling sick or dizzy. As I put fruit in my basket, I noticed him looking at me. When I dropped something, embarrassed, he picked it up and smiled at me, and asked my name. I told him.

"Kisagotami," he repeated, smiling again. "A pretty name for a pretty girl."

Two months later we were married. My father had been only too pleased to get rid of me. My new husband was a good man, but his family were only a little better off than my poor father, and I had to live with them as well as him. His mother was the worst – always complaining that I didn't work hard enough, no matter how much I tried to please her.

This all changed when I found that I was expecting a baby. Now it was more acceptable to have dizzy spells. People worried about me instead of shouting at me. And when the baby was born – a beautiful, dark-eyed boy – I was overjoyed. My husband was happy, I was happy, the family was happy. As a mother I had a purpose. I talked to other mothers in the market and we compared our children. As my boy grew, they all agreed that he was a strong and handsome boy, a credit to his parents. But in this world we can never tell what is to come – except for one thing.

One day, my boy went off to play with his friends in the forest. I was happily weaving a blanket at home when I heard an anxious cry.

"Kisagotami. Quick – it's your son!"

I don't know if you've ever felt that feeling – the dread that comes into your heart, and into your stomach, when you know something awful has happened. My son had been bitten by a snake. Men carried him into the house and laid him on the bed. He looked at me for a moment, and then his eyes closed for the last time. My son was dead.

A great wailing began. My husband's mother and sister buried their faces in their hands and wept. Neighbours tried to comfort me, but I was beside myself. My little boy looked just as if he was sleeping. There was no wound or any sign of illness, just a small red swelling on his ankle. Not really knowing what I was doing, I picked up his body and ran from the house. I went to every house in the village.

"Please, please, can you help me?" I pleaded. It seemed to me that there had to be some way to bring my son back to life. People offered me sympathy, but no magical cure that would do what I wanted. Some said, "There's no cure for death!" Others were frightened by my wild looks and cries and shut their doors.

When I had almost given in to complete despair, an old man came to his door and looked at me with great compassion. "There is a man who can help you," he said. My heart leaped! I had been right – there was a cure! I would pay any price – even give my own life if necessary. At last I could hope. The old man continued, "In the next village there is a man called Gautama. He is also called the Buddha. Go to him. Perhaps he can give you the medicine that you need."

I thanked the old man and set off. I walked through the night carrying my son's body. I should have been exhausted, but my desperate hope gave me strength. At noon of the next day I came to the neighbouring village. A large crowd was gathered, and I somehow knew that at the centre of this crowd was the man they called the Buddha. I pushed my way through the crowd until I stood before him and then I laid my child down.

"Great teacher," I begged. "Give me medicine for my child. Only you can help me." The crowd fell silent. As I waited for the Buddha to answer, the moment seemed to stretch into an eternity. The Buddha gazed into my eyes. I held my breath.

"Go to the city," he finally answered. "Go to every household and ask if it has ever been visited by death. If it has not, ask for a mustard seed. Bring me back all the mustard seeds you gather. Leave your son with me. I'll be waiting for you."

....

I felt so relieved. Everything was going to be all right after all. So I travelled to the city and began my search. At every house I asked, "Has death ever visited your home?" At every house the answer was the same. Everyone had lost someone – a father, a grandmother, a child… No one had been untouched by death. And as I listened to their tales of grief and lost loved ones, I began to learn: I was not alone. Others suffered just like me.

After several days, I returned empty-handed. Not one single mustard seed. I went to the Buddha and turned up my empty palms to him. He looked at me in silence as if I was his own lost child, and together we carried my son's body away.

What we have in common

ACTIVITY SHEET

PHOTOCOPIABLE

RE/Citizenship 11

CHAPTER 2

Bad Influences – Buddhism

TEACHERS' NOTES

This chapter is based on the Buddhist story 'The King's Elephant' and will need one or two lessons. The basic message is straightforward: people are influenced for better or worse by the company they keep. The story could be linked to 'Gobind Singh and the Donkey' (Chapter 14).

Themes
The influence of others; appearances

Citizenship Scheme of Work
- Unit 2 – Choices
- Unit 3 – Animals and us
- Unit 5 – Living in a diverse world

Aims
- To encourage children to consider the effects of the company they keep on their behaviour and outlook.

Resources
- The story 'The King's Elephant' (page 14)
- Copies of the questionnaires (pages 17 and 18)

Background
Buddhism warns us that we are influenced by the company we keep. If we are not yet strong in our Buddhist practice, we should therefore try to avoid the company of people who will have a bad influence on us by their example and by the kind of mood they generate. Conversely, we will be influenced positively by people who are calm, compassionate and morally upright. The story 'The King's Elephant' is designed to teach this doctrine.

Whole class starter
❑ Ask the children if anyone has ever said that someone else was a 'bad influence' on them. Ask if they know what this means. Explain that we often adopt the attitudes and behaviour of people around us, especially if we respect these people or want them to like and accept us. You could give the example of accent: a child who joins the school from another part of the country is likely to change their accent fairly quickly.

❑ Give out copies of the questionnaire on page 17. Tell children to fill it in, ticking the boxes to show how far they would be influenced by the behaviour shown. Then take an informal sample of answers as a starting point for discussion. This could be a whole-class discussion, or done in groups with the groups reporting back to the class.

❑ Before reading the story 'The King's Elephant', explain that this is a Buddhist story and that Buddhism emphasises the influence of the company we keep. You could add for older or more able children that the Chief Minister in the story is said to be the Buddha in a previous incarnation.

Activities
❑ Ask the children to fill out the questionnaire on page 18.

❑ The children could write a summary of the story or produce a picture version with captions. Both should end with a line

12 RE/Citizenship – Ages 9–11

beginning, 'The moral of this story is…'
You may need to explain this concept.

❑ The children could write a story based on 'The King's Elephant' about a boy or girl whose parents are worried because he or she starts behaving badly.

Differentiation

❑ To make the second questionnaire easier, adapt it so that the children just have to tick the box for the strongest influence for each of the items in column 1.

❑ Give the children a writing frame for the story based on 'The King's Elephant':

- X was the nicest boy/girl in the street. X's mum and dad were so proud…

- But one day, X's parents were surprised to see that…

- X's grandfather said, "I'll get to the bottom of this…"

- He followed X…

- "I've found the problem," he told X's parents. "It's that…"

- So, X's mum and dad said…

- X's mum and dad knew the problem was solved when…

❑ To give more challenge to the questionnaire activity, ask the children to provide examples of how they are influenced, or proof that they are not influenced, by the different people listed.

Extension

❑ The children could analyse and report on the results of the second questionnaire. These could be shown as a summary chart and displayed.

❑ They could further investigate one influence in the questionnaire; for example, television and films, devising a simple survey to find the most popular television programmes in the class and how far children think they are influenced by them.

Plenary session

❑ Review the results of the second questionnaire, either in detail after reading the results yourself, or simply by asking questions to get an overall picture, such as: 'Who put a 3 for "What you wear – teachers?"'

RE/Citizenship – Ages 9–11   13

The King's Elephant

There was once a king who lived in Varanasi, in India. Like many kings, he was very wealthy and had many fine possessions. He had a large palace with high and elegant towers commanding views over beautifully designed gardens with exotic plants and peacocks. He had swift Arabian horses in his stables and gold-trimmed chariots. He had so many servants that he had no idea himself how many he had. But his greatest pride and joy was his elephant, Mahilamukha.

This elephant was huge, with ears like giant rhubarb leaves and little beady eyes like black grapes. He was unusually intelligent too, and the King half believed that he understood every word spoken to him.

Mahilamukha not only had his own well furnished quarters, hung with the dazzling ceremonial head-dresses that he wore on special occasions. He also had his own mahout to look after his needs, clean out his bedding and bring him titbits. The mahout would take the elephant to the river to bathe in the mornings and play soothing music to him in the evenings to help him get to sleep. Having no wife or family, Mahilamukha was his greatest love, and he cared for the animal like a child.

One morning however, when the mahout brought Mahilamukha his breakfast, instead of the good-natured and affectionate animal that he was used to, he noticed a change. Mahilamukha was restless and deliberately nudged the well meaning man so that he fell over.

The next day the elephant was positively irritable, stamping, trumpeting and waving his trunk threateningly. What could be the matter? The mahout carefully examined the elephant for cuts and sores that might be annoying him, took his pulse, and even studied his dung for signs of sickness. Nothing seemed to be wrong – except that Mahilamukha had become a very bad tempered elephant.

The next day the mahout narrowly missed serious injury when Mahilamukha lunged at him, with a look in his beady eyes that could only be called murderous. Sadly, the man fetched some of the strongest servants, and with their help succeeded in tying up the huge beast so that he could not hurt anyone.

When the King heard about his favourite elephant's strange affliction, he sent his Chief Minister to find out what was causing it. This man was patient and clever, and decided to spend a night in the elephant's quarters to examine the animal more fully. He settled down quietly in a shadowy corner and was soon surprised to hear feet entering the building. Peering silently over the edge of the elephant's stall, he saw a gang of thieves sitting and talking.

"So," said the leader of the brigands, "It should be easy enough to get into the palace. But remember, if any servants appear, slit their throats before they can raise the alarm. Right! Meet here tomorrow evening, same time."

The Chief Minister waited for the men to leave, then went quickly to the King.

"Your Majesty," he began, "I believe I have found the cause of Mahilamukha's change of character."

"Really?" said the King, leaning forward eagerly. "What is it?"

"Mahilamukha's a clever elephant, but perhaps not quite as clever as we thought. A gang of thieves has been meeting in the elephant house to plan a robbery of your palace."

The King was shocked. "In my elephant house? Within the grounds of my palace?" he said, hardly believing his ears.

"I'm afraid so, Your Majesty. That in itself is bad enough, but I think Mahilamukha has been influenced by all their evil talk. Bad company has an effect on people."

"What do you suggest?"

"First, we must have the thieves rounded up and punished. They plan to meet again tomorrow. I'll get some guards onto it. But then we need to have honest, high minded holy men meet in the elephant house and discuss good deeds and kindness. With luck, that will influence Mahilamukha for the good."

The thieves were rounded up and the holy men installed in their place.

After one night, Mahilamukha's mahout noticed an improvement. After a week, the elephant became as well behaved and good tempered as he had ever been, gently picking up his mahout and placing him upon his back instead of threatening to trample him. Bad company had changed his character for the worse, but good company had cured him.

Name _____

Would you be influenced?

ACTIVITY SHEET 1

- ☐ Yes
- ☐ Probably
- ☐ Perhaps
- ☐ Probably not
- ☐ No

- ☐ Yes
- ☐ Probably
- ☐ Perhaps
- ☐ Probably not
- ☐ No

- ☐ Yes
- ☐ Probably
- ☐ Perhaps
- ☐ Probably not
- ☐ No

- ☐ Yes
- ☐ Probably
- ☐ Perhaps
- ☐ Probably not
- ☐ No

PHOTOCOPIABLE

RE/Citizenship 17

Name _____

What influences you?

In each box put a number from 0 to 3 to show how much you are influenced. **0** means no influence at all, **3** means a very strong influence.

For example, in the first row if you try to dress exactly like your friends, put a **3** under 'Friends', but if you think television and films have no influence on what you wear, put a **0** under 'TV & films'.

	Friends	Brothers & sisters	Parents	Teachers	TV & films
1 What you wear	☐	☐	☐	☐	☐
2 How you treat other people	☐	☐	☐	☐	☐
3 How you speak	☐	☐	☐	☐	☐
4 Attitude to crime	☐	☐	☐	☐	☐
5 Hobbies you have	☐	☐	☐	☐	☐
6 What hairstyle you have	☐	☐	☐	☐	☐
7 What you eat	☐	☐	☐	☐	☐

RE/Citizenship

PHOTOCOPIABLE

Family fairness – Christianity

TEACHERS' NOTES

This chapter, based around the story 'The Prodigal Son', is designed to work over one or two lessons. The story could be told alongside 'Monster-Slayer and Born-of-Water Visit Their Father' (Chapter 12), which also involves a father's treatment of his sons.

Themes

Contributing to the community, justice, forgiveness, parenthood

Citizenship scheme of work

- Unit 1 – Taking part
- Unit 2 – Choices
- Unit 4 – People who help us
- Unit 7 – Children's rights

Aims

To encourage children to consider:
- their personal contribution to family life and the life of any community (including the school) of which they are part;
- justice within the family and the community;
- what social safety nets there are to protect people from hardship.

Resources

- The story 'The Prodigal Son' (page 21)
- Copies of the photocopiable sheets on pages 25 and 26

Background

A key element of Christ's teachings is the forgiveness of sins: it is never too late to repent and receive the grace of God. The parable of 'The Prodigal Son' illustrates this point.

Whole class starter

❑ Give each child a copy of page 25. Ask the children to talk about the pictures and what they show, and then to put them in order as shown on the sheet. Discuss their views. For example, should they be expected to tidy their room but not clean the car? Why? Ask them to list ways in which they help their parents, carers or others.

❑ Before reading the story 'The Prodigal Son', tell the children that it is a parable – a story said to have been told by Jesus – found in the New Testament of the Bible (Luke 15: 11–32). Explain that 'prodigal' means wasteful or reckless: someone who spends all their money without a thought for how they will live tomorrow is prodigal.

❑ Now read the story.

Activities

❑ Ask the class whether they think Samuel made the right choice in leaving home in the first place. Give them each a copy of page 26 and ask them to write down what they think are the pros and cons of each of his possible choices.

❑ Set up a hot-seating session. Say to the class: 'Imagine Samuel, Luke and their father and mother were here. Make a list of questions you would like to ask each of them about how they were feeling at different times in the story.' Ask for four children to volunteer to take on the four roles. The rest of the class

should then take turns putting their questions to the relevant characters, for example:
Q – Luke, how did you feel when your brother left home?
A – I thought, 'Good riddance to bad rubbish!' He was useless on the farm. I didn't think Dad should have given him any money, but at least then he'd be out of our way for good.

❏ Ask the class, 'When Samuel was starving and penniless, did he deserve any help?' The children could discuss and write a paragraph about who deserves help, and who is helped, in the present day.

Differentiation

❏ You could make the hot-seating activity easier by giving children questions on cards. In addition to the one given, they could ask:

- Luke, how did you feel when your brother came back and your father ordered a feast to celebrate?

- Father, can you explain why you gave a feast for Samuel when he came back broke, yet never did the same for Luke?

- Samuel, now that you've come back penniless and been made welcome, are you going to change your ways and work hard?

- Mother, how did you feel when Samuel went away? How do you feel now that he's back?

- Mother, do you feel that your husband was right to welcome Samuel back and have a feast for him?

❏ A more challenging task would be to write about how far community help should depend on how deserving people are – for example, should drug addicts or released prisoners receive help? Encourage children to consider the consequences for society if these people receive no help.

Extension

❏ To follow on from the hot-seating activity, children could rewrite the story from the point of view of one of the characters. Note that the mother's account will require most imagination, as she doesn't make a personal appearance in the story.

Plenary session

❏ Take a vote on whether the father behaves fairly to his two sons when Samuel comes home, and discuss different children's reasons for voting the way they have.

The Prodigal Son

A wealthy farmer had two grown-up sons. He loved them both equally, but they were as different as stone and sand.

Luke, the elder son, was serious minded. He worked hard on the farm. He planted vines, he inspected the sheep, cut out the rot from their hooves, and repaired the stables. He kept an eye on the hired workers and reported them to his father if he suspected any of them of shirking or stealing. He followed his father's instructions even when there was something else he would much rather be doing.

Luke's brother Samuel on the other hand, was a cheerful, happy-go-lucky young man. He'd sooner be drinking wine than planting the vines, and although he would happily share a joke with his father's hired workers, he wasn't interested in the standard of their work. When Luke asked, 'When are you going to start acting responsibly and do your share of the work around here?' Samuel replied, 'When are you going to lighten up? There's more to life than sick sheep and the price of nails!'

Samuel had an easy smile and was always ready to stop whatever he was doing to chat with travelling sheep traders and craftsmen. They told him stories of other lands, where people lived differently. He heard about wild parties, with flowing wine and dancing girls and he thought to himself: 'What am I waiting for?'

'Father,' Samuel began one day, 'I've been thinking. You have just two sons, and when you die – which of course I hope won't be for years – the farm and all your money will go to both of us. That's right, isn't it?'

'If I die before your mother, I trust you'll look after her, son – but, yes, the farm will be yours and Luke's. Why?'

'Well, I was thinking that if I had my half of your wealth now, I could go off into the big wide world and make my fortune. You'd be proud of me. I'd come back a rich man with a herd of camels and fifty servants!'

'Things out in the big wide world may not be that simple,' said the father. 'But if you've thought long and hard about this…'

'I have, honestly – long and hard,' said Samuel, trying to sound as though he really had.

His father clapped him on the shoulder. 'Then you shall have your half. I like a young man with initiative! Of course, I may have to sell a few sheep to raise the cash, but that's all right.'

When Luke heard the news, he was dismayed. 'Father,' he said. 'I hear you're going to give Samuel his inheritance.'

'That's right, son. He wants to go off and make his fortune.'

'I'm afraid he may just make a fool of himself!'

'Do you question my judgement, Son?'

'No, Father. You know I always respect your decision, but…' The conversation was over.

Not long after this conversation, Samuel left with his money. His mother wept. His father embraced him. His brother shook his head.

A few weeks later, a passing camel herder stopped at the farm and asked if he could water his camels. They were thirsty from a long trek across the desert. Luke noticed an emerald glinting on the camel herder's hand.

'Where did you get that ring?' he asked.

'A generous young man gave it to me. Well, in truth, I won it from him playing dice.' He laughed. 'A fine young man. Free with his money. A man who knew how to enjoy life. Looked like you but with fewer worries!'

Luke recognised the ring. It was his brother's – part of his share of the family wealth.

Two months later, a spice merchant came by. He had seen Samuel in a market at a town across the desert. Samuel, the merchant reported, was liked and admired – because he spent money as though it were sand running through his fingers. Naturally, he had many hangers-on, who hoped that some of his wealth would spill onto them. The local girls were especially fond of him, because he bought them bracelets and paid them compliments.

After this there were occasional reports of Samuel but they came further and further apart. His father began to fear that he would never see his son again.

Samuel, meanwhile, was still popular with everyone he met, while his money lasted. He travelled further and further, always finding new delights to try. But one day, a year after he had left home, it dawned on him – he was no longer wealthy. In fact, he had hardly a shekel left to his name. The thought made him feel hungry and he went to a shop where he knew the shopkeeper.

'My good friend,' Samuel said with a smile. 'Let me have some bread and some of that goat's cheese, as well as a few olives and a skin of wine.'

'Coming up!' said the shopkeeper, starting to collect the items. 'But I'm afraid prices have risen. This famine is really starting to hit home.'

'Yes… well the thing is,' Samuel said hesitantly, 'I'll have to pay you tomorrow.'

The shopkeeper leaned on the counter. 'My friend, I need the money now. Times are hard. I'm sorry – no money, no food.'

Samuel was stunned. He went quickly out into the street and started to walk to his lodgings. There, he found his landlord carrying off his possessions.

'Hey, those are my clothes – and that's my jewel box!' said Samuel indignantly.

'You haven't paid the rent for two months. These things will barely cover it,' the landlord replied.

There was nothing for it, Samuel thought. He'd have to get a job. He went to one farmer after another, but times were hard and no one was hiring help. At last he found a man who needed someone to feed his pigs in the fields. He paid very little, but Samuel was desperate. As he threw bean pods to the grunting pigs, he was tempted to eat some of them himself, but he was afraid of being spotted by the farmer and fired. He asked passing travellers for food, but the famine had put paid to any hope of charity.

After a week of this Samuel was exhausted and half-starved. Lying awake one night in the straw beside two donkeys and a sick goat, he wondered how things were at his father's farm. All the farm workers there got a square meal each day. No-one starved or had to wear rags.

The next day, Samuel went to the farmer and said he was going home. The man gave him a few shekels and a piece of hard cheese for the journey. Samuel walked, or hitched a ride with a camel train when he could. Everywhere he saw signs of famine; children as thin as a knife edge, corn bins empty. Miles and miles, weeks and weeks passed. Finally Samuel neared his home country, and then his father's farm.

'Master, master! Your son has returned. He is limping along the track. He looks tired and thin, master!' The servant pointed in the direction of the track.

The old man, master of the house, said a silent prayer of thanks. 'God has blessed me. My son has returned at last!'

To his servant he announced 'Ezekiel, kill that calf we've been fattening up for a feast. We will celebrate my son's return. Call up the musicians. My son has returned!'

As Samuel approached the house, his father came out to meet him, along with many of the servants. The old man hugged his son. 'How thin you've become! You need a good meal, my boy!'

But Samuel said to his father, 'Father, I have sinned against God and against you. I threw away your money on worthless things. Let me work in your fields for a hired man's wage.'

'Nonsense, my boy,' said the father. 'You'll have nothing but the best. I'm just grateful that God has returned you to me.'

Out in the fields, Samuel's brother Luke was working hard as usual. He called out to a servant who had gone to fetch water, 'What's all the noise for?'

When he learned the reason, he strode angrily to his father.

'Father,' he said, 'I worked obediently for you for years. I never complained. Yet you never gave me so much as a skinny goat to roast with my friends. Yet my brother spends all your money on gambling, wine and dancing girls, and now when he crawls home for a hand out, you kill the fatted calf for him to celebrate! Is that fair?'

'Son,' said the old man, 'You are always with me, an obedient son, and all that I have is yours. But this other son was as good as dead to me, and now he has come back to life. He was lost and now he is found.'

Name _____

Being helpful

Which of these things do you ever do to be helpful? Put a tick for each one.
In the empty box, draw a picture of another way in which you are helpful.
Then number the pictures to show how far you feel you **should** do them.
Use **1** for the one you most feel you should do and **6** for the least.

PHOTOCOPIABLE

RE/Citizenship 25

Name _____

Samuel's choices

Think about Samuel's possible choices. For each one, write down the 'pros' (things that make it a good idea) and the 'cons' (things that make it a bad idea).

I could stay here and work hard on the farm.

Pros:

Cons:

I could stay here and take it easy-like I do now!

Pros:

Cons:

I could go away and start a used camel business, and save all my profits.

Pros:

Cons:

I could go away and spend my money on having a great time. You're only young once!

Pros:

Cons:

26 RE/Citizenship
PHOTOCOPIABLE

Loyalty and the law – Christianity

TEACHER'S NOTES

> This chapter looks at the story of Peter's betrayal of Jesus. It could be spread over one or two lessons, and could be coupled with the story of 'The Five Beloved Ones' (Chapter 13), which also involves trust in a spiritual leader.

Themes

Trust, betrayal, loyalty, courage, non-violence, the law

Citizenship scheme of work

- Unit 2 – Choices
- Unit 5 – Living in a diverse world
- Unit 8 – How do rules and laws affect me?
- Unit 12 – Moving on

Aims

To encourage children to consider:
- how far we should trust leaders;
- standing up for one's beliefs;
- loyalty to a group;
- the role of law in protecting our society.

Resources

- The story 'The Betrayal of Jesus' (page 29)
- Copies of the photocopiable sheet on page 32

Background

According to the New Testament, Christ willingly allowed himself to be arrested and crucified in order to save humankind from their sins. He also encouraged his disciples to take his words on trust, and preached non-violence. All these things are shown in the story.

Whole class starter

❑ If possible, begin with a trust exercise. One child stands closely surrounded by four others. when all the other children are ready, the child in the centre shuts his or her eyes and falls in any direction. (For safety reasons make sure an adult always oversees this activity.)

❑ Ask, 'What is trusting someone? Who do you trust to tell you how to behave?' Ask the children to arrange the following in order of whom they trust most, or to come up with their own list: teacher; mother; father; friend; brother or sister; police; doctor; someone on television. Ask the children to work in groups to discuss the order they have chosen and their reasons for it. For example, has this person usually been right in the past?

❑ Finally, ask the groups to discuss how far they would trust each person. For example, if encouraged by this person, would they: wear a new sweatshirt; swallow a tablet; jump out of the window?

❑ Before reading the story 'The Betrayal of Jesus', tell the children that it is from the New Testament of the Bible. Now read the story.

Activities

❑ Ask the children to retell the story from the point of view of one of the disciples – for example, Peter or Judas.

❏ Ask the children to design a 'Wanted' poster about Jesus, to suggest what crimes the authorities accused him of.

❏ Organise the children into groups to discuss the following questions:

- Should Jesus have run away if he knew that he was in trouble?
- Should Jesus have defended himself in any way?
- What possible reasons could Judas have had for betraying Jesus?
- Would Peter be right to deny knowing Jesus in order to save himself? (This is what happens later.)

❏ Children could discuss whether it is always right to obey the law, then write a story exploring this question.

❏ Give each child a copy of page 32. Go through Judas's thoughts with the class, then ask the children to write their own version of a letter he might have written explaining his betrayal of Jesus.

Differentiation

❏ Give children a simple writing frame to help with the storytelling activity:

- When we went into the room for the Passover meal, I felt…

- At first, the meal seemed to be going well, but then…

- When we reached the Mount of Olives, I felt so tired…

- When Jesus saw the crowd approaching, I…

Extension

❏ Read the Bible's different versions of the story with the class – see Matthew 26: 17-50, Luke 22: 1-48 and John 18: 1–11. Compare these versions with the version given here.

❏ Read Matthew 26:69–75 for Peter's denial of Jesus.

Plenary session

❏ Ask children if they think Judas made the right choice. If not, why not? What about Peter? Tell them that Jesus was right when he said that Peter would deny him. (See extension above.) Was Peter right to do this?

The Betrayal of Jesus

Jerusalem was restless. Passover, the festival at which the Jews celebrated the time when God saved them from slavery in Egypt, was approaching. This was a special time, a holy time.

A man called Jesus had been gathering bigger and bigger crowds, telling stories that left the people spellbound, performing miracles and calling himself Son of God and King of the Jews. Some people wondered if this extraordinary man was going to save his people from Roman rule. The Jewish high priests were worried. This upstart – the son of a humble carpenter – was a threat to their authority. He would have to go.

Meanwhile, in a poor part of the city, the followers of Jesus gathered around him. He waved two of his closest disciples over.

'John, Peter,' he said. 'Go and prepare the Passover meal for us all.'

'Where should we prepare it, Master?' asked Peter, anxious to please.

Jesus spoke with that air of mystery that he often had. 'Go into the city. You'll meet a man carrying a jar of water. Follow him. When he goes into a house, find the owner and tell him that the Teacher wants to know where the guest room is in which we shall eat the Passover meal. He'll show you a large, furnished upstairs room. That's the place.'

That evening, Jesus and all the disciples went to the house and went upstairs. Peter and John had prepared a simple meal. There were thirteen places set around a long table. Jesus sat at the centre of the table. He said prayers and then they all began to eat. Jesus was quiet at first. Then he spoke to his disciples: 'I very much wanted to share this Passover meal with you before my time of suffering.' The disciples exchanged worried glances. John, sitting next to Jesus, touched his arm.

Jesus made a gesture which seemed to say, 'Don't worry,' and almost in the same movement he took up a loaf of rye bread and began to break pieces, passing them round to the disciples. As he did so, he told them, 'Take this and eat it. This is my body.' Again, the disciples exchanged glances, but they obediently did as Jesus told them.

PHOTOCOPIABLE

Next, Jesus poured wine from an earthenware jar into a large goblet and passed it round, saying, 'Drink this wine, all of you. It is my blood, poured out for the forgiveness of sins. I will not drink wine again before I drink it with you in heaven.' Now a very serious mood fell on the disciples. What did Jesus mean, they asked themselves. Was their guide and teacher going to die? But there was a bigger shock to come.

'Truly, I tell you,' said Jesus, 'that tonight one of you here will betray me.' Some cried 'No, no!' Others quickly leaned towards Jesus, asking fearfully, 'Is it me, Lord?'

Jesus said to them all, 'He who has dipped his hand in the dish with me will betray me.' He smiled sadly and nodded, brushing aside their disbelief. Then he looked straight at Judas, sitting at the end of the table. Judas looked away in discomfort, refusing to meet the eyes of Jesus. For he knew that he was the one who would betray Jesus.

The meal ended in a very different mood from the one in which it had begun, though there was no change in Jesus, who had been serious from the start. They left the house and went to the Garden of Gethsemane on the Mount of Olives. Here there was relief from the bustle of the city, and cool breezes softened the heat of the Jerusalem night. Jesus sat on a fallen olive branch, with the disciples all around him.

'After tonight,' he said, 'you will all fall away from me. It is prophesied that you will all be scattered.'

'No, Lord,' said Peter, the sturdy fisherman. 'I will always remain loyal to you, come what may!'

'Even you, Peter,' Jesus insisted. 'Before the cock crows in the morning, you will deny three times that you even know me.'

Peter looked confused, but held his peace out of respect for Jesus.

Jesus seemed tired and distracted. 'Stay awake with me while I pray tonight,' he asked his disciples. And he walked a little distance away to another part of the garden and prayed to God that he might escape the suffering that was soon to come.

'None the less, Lord,' he added, 'if it is your will, then so be it.' He prayed so hard that beads of sweat broke out on his forehead, and an angel came to strengthen him in his hour of need.

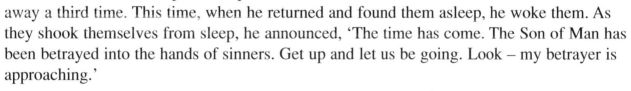

When Jesus returned an hour later the disciples were all asleep, stretched out on the ground. 'You could not even stay awake with me for a little while,' he said, in a voice that was sad but forgiving.

Again Jesus went away to pray. An hour later, he returned to find the disciples asleep as before. He went away a third time. This time, when he returned and found them asleep, he woke them. As they shook themselves from sleep, he announced, 'The time has come. The Son of Man has been betrayed into the hands of sinners. Get up and let us be going. Look – my betrayer is approaching.'

The disciples looked where Jesus was pointing – all eleven of them, because the twelfth disciple, Judas, was approaching in the grey pre-dawn light, bringing with him a large group of men. At their head were Jewish priests and elders, wrapped in their robes of authority, but the men swarming behind them were armed with swords and clubs. They were all eager to take part in the arrest of the man who called himself King of the Jews.

At a sign from a high priest, the crowd stopped. Judas spoke quietly to the priest: 'The one I kiss is Jesus.' Then he stepped forward and walked under the olive trees towards Jesus and kissed him on the cheek in greeting.

Jesus gazed at him with sorrow and pity. 'Judas, would you betray the Son of Man with a kiss?'

Judas made no answer. Instead he stood in fear and confusion, already beginning to feel in his stomach the horror of what he had done. Then he was roughly shoved aside as the mob seized Jesus to carry him off for trial.

Name _____

Judas

ACTIVITY SHEET 1

RE/Citizenship PHOTOCOPIABLE

Honesty and fairness – Hinduism

TEACHERS' NOTES

> This chapter is based on the Hindu story 'Lakshmi and the Wise Washerwoman'. The story could be linked to 'King Hansa' (Chapter 9) or 'The Monkey King' (Chapter 6). The section is designed to work over one or two lessons.

Themes
Honesty rewarded, expectations, choices, poverty and wealth

Citizenship scheme of work
- Unit 7 – Rights
- Unit 9 – Respect for property

Aims
- To encourage children to think about the connections between fairness, honesty and respect for property.

Resources
- The story 'Lakshmi and the Wise Washerwoman' (page 35)
- Copies of the photocopiable sheet on page 39

Background
Most Hindus view their many gods as expressions of Brahman, or godhead. Lakshmi, the goddess of prosperity, featured in this chapter's story, is associated with the festival of Divali (Diwali), as is Kali, goddess of destruction and renewal.

Divali (from Sanskrit dipavali, row of lights), the 'festival of lights', celebrates the triumph of good over evil, light over darkness. It usually falls in October or November. The festival, like Lakshmi, is associated with prosperity. The story of 'Lakshmi and the Wise Washerwoman' expresses the belief that wealth is earned by good deeds. The washerwoman behaves honestly and is rewarded by Poverty being banished from her home for seven generations. This could also reflect the Hindu belief in reincarnation and karma. Note that karma is often confused with punishment for sins. In fact it is simply an energy created by good or bad deeds and passed on from one incarnation to the next.

Whole class starter
❑ Ask the children to list their three most treasured possessions. These don't have to be expensive and they cannot be people or pets. Tell them that the possessions could be of 'sentimental value' and explain what this means. Ask a few children to explain their choices to the class, then divide the class into small groups. In their groups they should:

- decide which of the three things they would be most upset to lose;
- see if they would be prepared to swap any of their listed possessions for something belonging to another child in the group;
- think of one thing that they don't have but would really like to have. (This could be a realistic choice, like a bicycle, or an imaginary one, like a pet triceratops.)

❑ Ask the class if it is fair for some people to have more than others. Ask them to compare: someone who works hard and earns the money to buy something; someone who is given a house by a rich relative; and someone like a footballer who earns a lot of money because they have a special skill.

❑ Give the children copies of the photocopiable sheet on page 39, which shows the choices someone could make if they found a wallet full of money. Ask them to discuss what they would do in this situation. If everyone says 'Hand it in to the police,' point out that the wallet looks expensive. Does this make a difference? Does it make a difference if the person who finds the wallet is very poor? When the discussion draws to a close, tell children that this situation is based on a true story. A young man found the wallet on a train. Inside the wallet he found information about the owner including his job and address. The owner was a bursar – somebody who looks after money – at a university. The young man kept the money but sent the wallet back to the bursar with an unsigned note saying, 'I hope you look after the university's money better than your own.' Ask the children what they think about this.

❏ Before reading the story 'Lakshmi and the Wise Washerwoman', explain its context (see Background). Now read the story.

Activities

❏ Brainstorm words that could describe the king and queen. If necessary, start the children off with one or two of the following, explaining unfamiliar words:
King: rich, devoted, generous, loving, soft hearted, fair, indulgent
Queen: spoilt, vain, demanding, childish, beautiful, appreciative

❏ Is the king right to be so generous to the queen? Is he a good king? If necessary, point out that he hardly knows that the slum area of his realm exists. Is it the queen's fault that she is vain and spoilt? Can it be a disadvantage to be born into a rich family?

❏ Talk about what 'prosperity' is. Why did the washerwoman choose prosperity rather than the money the king offered her?

❏ Choose small groups to take on the roles of different characters in the story. The groups take turns to be in the 'hot seat' while the rest of the class ask them questions. Start them off with suggestions along these lines:

King Why do you always give the Queen expensive presents?
Queen How did you feel when you lost the necklace?
Washerwoman Why didn't you keep the necklace?
Poverty Why did you stay with the washerwoman?
Lakshmi What did you think when you saw no lights?

❏ Ask the children to work in groups to discuss the washerwoman's choice and what they would have done in her place.

Differentiation

❏ For the brainstorming activity, include some red herrings among the words you suggest; for example, 'evil', 'ugly', 'mean', 'careless'. Ask the children to spot the words that don't apply to the king or queen.

❏ Older or more able children could write about 'How the world can be made a fairer place' or about what they think Lakshmi and Poverty represent in the story.

Extension

❏ Children could act out scenes from the story. They could extend and adapt the scene in which the king asks the queen what she wants for Divali. He could offer a series of fantastic gifts, each of which she rejects until she gets to one she wants. These could be modern gifts or in keeping with the setting of the story. The children could also act out a similar scene with the roles reversed – a devoted queen and a spoiled king.

❏ The children could use the Internet to research Divali and the role of the goddess Lakshmi in Hindu myth.

Plenary session

❏ Introduce the concept of the story having a 'moral'. Ask children to write a sentence saying what they think the moral is, or try to reach a consensus through discussion.

Lakshmi and the Wise Washerwoman

Once, in ancient India, a king and queen lived in a beautiful palace. The King was as devoted to his queen as any man could be. He was also fabulously wealthy. The Queen was vain. She liked to gaze at herself in mirrors and hated to think that other women might be more beautiful or more finely dressed than she was. The Queen was also used to having her own way. Ever since she was a little princess, she had always been given exactly what she wanted by everyone around her, and now she was really rather spoilt. So every year at Divali she asked her husband for presents that most people would only ever dream of owning. And every year he did everything he could to obtain them for her, whatever the price, the difficulty or the danger.

'What can I get you for Divali this year?' the King asked the Queen as she lay resting on a bed of pink silk cushions, wafted by exotic perfumes and fanned by feathers from rare birds.

'Mmm…' she considered, 'Perhaps jewellery.' She held a hand mirror up to her face and tilted her head to one side. 'A necklace, I think. Let me see: I have rubies, diamonds… but no pearls. Good. I'd like a pearl necklace.'

'Of course, my love,' said the King, stroking the Queen's neck affectionately. 'A string of the finest pearls – you'll look lovely in it.'

'I know. But I want to look even lovelier! Not just one string. Get me a seven-string pearl necklace. A nice one.'

The King gave orders for men to be dispatched to the far corners of the world, to find pearl-divers to seek out the biggest and most perfect pearls from all the seven seas. At length, and just in time for Divali, the pearls were gathered up and strung – one string from each of the seven seas. When the King fastened the necklace on the Queen's slender neck and handed her a looking glass, she was delighted. She turned her pretty head this way and that, and felt as if the beautiful lustre of the pearls was in fact her own. The King gazed and sighed appreciatively.

The Queen was still wearing the necklace when she went to the river to bathe next day. Accompanied by her handmaidens, she passed through the palace gardens, out into the royal deer park, and soon came to the river. At a secluded spot, guarded by palace servants, she took off her clothes. She was just about to dive in when a handmaiden said, 'Your Majesty…' and pointed to the necklace.

PHOTOCOPIABLE

RE/Citizenship 35

'Oh, yes,' said the Queen. 'Here, look after it for me.' And she plunged into the cooling water. The handmaidens watched the necklace, but the bathing place was guarded and surely no harm could come to it here. As the women talked and picked flowers a shadow flitted over them. Before they knew it, a large black crow had plucked the shimmering necklace up in his beak and flown away with it.

The handmaidens cried out in shock and horror. A few tried to chase after the bird, but of course the pursuit was hopeless. The clamour brought the Queen back to the bank.

'Where's my necklace?' she asked immediately, a note of threat in her voice.

'Your Majesty… a crow. The necklace is gone.' The Queen could barely believe this catastrophe. In moments, her disbelief turned to grief and anger. Why hadn't the young women guarded the precious necklace properly? Why hadn't they caught the crow? Big salty tears of powerless rage burst from her, like pearls from the seven seas.

When the Queen reported the story to the King, he was disappointed but he reassured the Queen: 'I'll get you an even better one – eight or nine strings!'

'No, that one was perfect. You must find that necklace,' replied the still tearful Queen. So the King sent out criers and messengers all across the land offering a big reward to anyone who found the necklace. And all over the land, children climbed trees to look in crows' nests and people studied every crow that passed overhead to see if it was carrying something bright and gleaming.

The crow, however, had not flown to its nest. Instead, it had flown high and far, across the city to a slum area far from the royal palace. The King and Queen had barely heard of this district. They had certainly never visited it. Its streets were narrow and filthy. Its houses were small, in poor repair and crowded in on each other, seeming to jostle for air and space.

The crow circled over the slum, dropped the necklace on a poor woman's doorstep, then flew off.

This woman made her living by washing other people's clothes. There was barely enough room in her hut for her and the piles of laundry, yet she also shared it with a skinny old woman whose name was Poverty. The pair did not like each other much, but they put up with each other. The washerwoman could not remember a time when Poverty had not lived with her. Poverty went everywhere with her. When the crow dropped the necklace, the two were out together collecting clothes. They heard a herald announcing the King's promised reward.

'Ha!' sneered Poverty. 'These kings and queens have more money than sense!' But the washerwoman had already started to dream of owning a necklace like that herself. Naturally, she thought she must still be dreaming when she arrived at her house and found the necklace in a heap on the doorstep. She considered putting it on, but she had no mirror to look in. So, instead, she told Poverty she had to go somewhere, scooped the necklace into an inconspicuous old shopping bag, and headed for the King's palace.

She had difficulty at first getting the palace guards to notice her. But when she gave them a glimpse of the necklace, their eyes popped out of their heads and they gave her a personal escort to the King. He was astonished to see the necklace again, and in the rough (but clean) hands of a poor washerwoman.

'You're poor but honest, I can see. And your honesty will be rewarded – not just by the gods, but by me.' And he clicked his fingers to a servant who quickly brought a bag of gold coins from the royal treasury. This was enough money to keep a washerwoman in luxury for the rest of her life. With a final wave of thanks, the King was already turning away, imagining how happy the Queen would be when he surprised her with the necklace for a second time.

But the washerwoman spoke again.

'I don't want your money, Your Majesty,' she said.

'What? But it's yours, really. I've got lots!'

'I had something else in mind – a special favour to ask of you. It's Divali, the festival of light. If you would be kind to a poor washerwoman, please issue an order that all the lamps in your land should be put out, except for mine.'

'Very well,' said the King. He was puzzled, but he immediately gave the order. Even in his own palace, servants started to put away the lamps.

The washerwoman hurried home, buying lamps on the way. She lit them and arranged them outside her humble home, around the same doorstep on which the gleaming treasure had been dropped earlier that day. When night fell, the washerwoman went out and looked around. Everywhere was dark except at the entrance to her home! Needless to say, she felt rather special.

Meanwhile, Lakshmi the goddess of prosperity had left the heavens to begin her yearly Divali tour, in which she blessed all the homes lit with lamps in her honour with prosperity. But instead of a thousand flickering lamps, she saw a blanket of darkness spread across the land. Everywhere was thick night – except for one faint glimmer of light in the far distance.

Tired and baffled, the goddess arrived finally at the source of the light – the washerwoman's hut. Through its one window she could see a room brightly lit by more lamps. She banged on the door.

'Let me in, let me in!'

'I'll let you in on one condition – that you stay with me for seven generations.'

Just then, the washerwoman spied Poverty trying to creep out by the back door. But the washerwoman got there first and locked it.

'Let me out! Let me out!' pleaded Poverty.

'I'll let you out on one condition – that you stay away from me for seven generations.'

'Yes, anything!' cried Poverty. 'I can't stand the light of Lakshmi. I couldn't live in the same house as her.'

'Anything!' cried Lakshmi. 'I must have light!'

So the washerwoman quickly let Poverty out of the back door and let Lakshmi in at the front door.

And so the wise washerwoman's home was blessed with prosperity for seven generations. She and her children – right down to her great, great, great, great grandchildren – always had plenty of everything.

What would you do?

Groups and leaders – Hinduism

TEACHERS' NOTES

This chapter is based on the Hindu story 'The Monkey King'. The work could be spread over one or two lessons. The story would work well told alongside 'King Hansa' (Chapter 9) or 'Lakshmi and the Wise Washerwoman' (Chapter 5).

Themes

Kingship, trust, respect, compassion, self sacrifice

Citizenship scheme of work

- Unit 1 – Taking part
- Unit 3 – Animals and us
- Unit 5 – Living in a diverse world
- Unit 10 – Local democracy

Aims

- To encourage children to think about: group effort; leadership; self sacrifice for the good of the community; and caring for the environment.

Resources

- The story 'The Monkey King' (page 42)
- Copies of the photocopiable sheet on page 45
- A mango and a long rope (optional)

Background

The story of 'The Monkey King' is also told by Buddhists, with the Monkey King himself seen as a previous incarnation of the Buddha. The virtue shown by the Monkey King in fulfilling his duty of care towards the people he leads is a Hindu virtue, but would equally be applauded by many other religions. The same could be said for the Monkey King's claim that 'it is love, not power, that makes a great king.'

Whole class starter

❏ Give out copies of page 45 and ask the children to look at the pictures of leaders. Ask them to comment on the different styles of leadership shown. Ask: 'What is each leader doing?'; 'Is any style better or more useful than the others?'; 'Are there other ways in which leaders behave, not shown here?' Guide the class towards realising that the pictures illustrate:

- helping to bring out and use team members' strengths;
- leading by consensus – helping to reach an agreement;
- leading by example – and being the first to take a risk;
- leading by force of character, or even threat.

❏ Divide the class into four or five groups. Give each group a jigsaw puzzle. Appoint one person in each group as leader, and one as observer. The group has five minutes to do as much of the puzzle as they can. The observer's job is to watch what goes on and how the group works to do the puzzle. After five minutes, ask each observer how the group worked together and how the leader led the group. Ask whether the leader behaved like any of the leaders in the pictures. Did the leader do as much work as the others? Did everyone do what the leader said? (Suitable alternative tasks to the jigsaw include building a model, drawing a group picture to represent the school, or a map of the area.)

❑ Before reading 'The Monkey King', tell the class that it is a very old Hindu story about leadership and working together as a group.

Activities

❑ As a class, discuss the answers to these questions, to check comprehension:

- What was the monkeys' secret treasure? (The mango tree – show the class a mango if possible.)

- Why was there always a risk that human beings would find out about the tree? (It overhung the River Ganges.)

- What did the monkeys do to prevent people finding out about the mangoes? (They ate all the flowers on the side of the tree that overhung the river, so that they couldn't turn into fruit. Check that the children understand this process.)

- Who took the mango to the king? (Fishermen)

- How did the Monkey King save his people? (He leapt to a tree on the opposite river bank, tied a vine to his ankle, jumped back and grabbed a branch of the mango tree; but the vine was too short so he had to hang on while the other monkeys used him as a bridge. You can demonstrate most of this using a child, a rope and a stretch of floor to represent the river. The key thing for children to understand is that the vine was too short.)

- Why was the king impressed?

❑ Point out to the children that for years the monkeys kept the fruit safe by a 'joint effort'. This involves 'taking part'. Tell them to draw or list at least four ways in which they have taken part in a joint effort. This is a good opportunity to remember class or school achievements, such as a school play, a sports team, or decorating the classroom.

❑ Ask the children to imagine that the monkeys have launched a 'Save Our Tree' campaign. In groups, they could plan a protest, design a poster, produce an information leaflet about the tree and why the monkeys have a right to its fruits, or write a short campaign speech.

❑ Tell the children to write and illustrate a paragraph about a real or imaginary leader whom they admire. They must say what makes this person a good leader.

Differentiation

❑ Give visual clues for the comprehension activity, such as a mango, a flower or a picture of a fish.

❑ Let the children think of just one or two 'taking part' examples.

❑ Give the children some initial ideas for points to make in the 'Save Our Tree' campaign: the monkeys were there first; humans might destroy the tree, especially if they fight over it.

❑ Give examples of types of leaders, such as sports captains, politicians, or leaders in a school or home setting.

Extension

❑ The children could find out about local environmental issues and groups and find out how decisions are made locally.

❑ They could identify ways in which they would like their school or local environment to be improved or protected.

❑ For a more challenging activity, children could put the different leadership styles given on the copiable sheet (page 45) in order of their personal preference, then write about why they have chosen this order.

Plenary session

❑ Lead the children in brainstorming a list of leadership qualities. You could write on the board: 'A good leader…' then add actions, for example '…makes the most of people's strengths.'

RE/Citizenship – Ages 9–11 41

The Monkey King

The Himalayas are the highest mountains in the world. Their dazzling, snow topped peaks look down with a cool and distant gaze on the hot valleys far below. Just below the snow line, crystal streams of meltwater spring up and tumble down towards the foothills. And by the time they get there they have joined up with so many other streams that they have become rushing rivers. The River Ganges is one of these rivers.

At a place where the River Ganges begins to slow its rapid descent to the plains where the cities of men were built, there once lived a huge tribe of monkeys: 80,000 of them. They were ruled over by a wise Monkey King. At the centre of his kingdom, beside the pure-flowing river, there grew a beautiful tree. Its trunk and branches were strong and elegant. Its perfumed flowers delighted the monkeys in the spring. Its large, spreading leaves gave them shade in the noonday heat of summer. But in the autumn, the tree produced the gift most treasured by the monkeys – a crop of large, sweetly delicious mangoes that continued for weeks. No other tree in the area – or perhaps in all India – grew fruit like this.

The tree was a wonderful blessing, but some blessings carry a price. The Monkey King, in his wisdom, warned his people that if anyone else heard about the mango tree, they might want its fruit all for themselves. He knew how greedy human beings could be, and he worried that if men heard about the tree they would come with weapons and drive the monkeys away in order to claim the fruit for themselves. This was a particular worry because the tree's branches hung out far over the river. If one of the fabulous fruit ever fell into the river and was carried downstream to the land of men, and if they once tasted it, they would be sure to come looking for the tree.

For this reason, on the Monkey King's orders, every spring the monkeys ate the blossom from those branches that hung out over the river, so that no fruit could grow from them. And when the fruit came, they searched again just in case they had missed a flower somewhere and it had now produced a fruit that might fall into the river.

Perhaps it was the will of the gods, or perhaps the monkeys became careless, but one year a flower hanging far out over the river escaped attention. It opened its inviting petals to a bee, who pollinated it so that a fruit began to grow. Hidden from view by the leaves, the fruit grew large and ripe, like a setting sun. One day, at the moment of perfect ripeness, as a gentle breeze stirred the tree, the fruit fell from the branch and splashed heavily into the flowing river below. It was carried, bobbing swiftly at first, then gliding at a more leisurely pace, until it reached the plains where the river spread out like a wide and sinuous road. Here it landed in the net of a group of fishermen.

'I saw it first. I'm going to take the first bite!' said one.

'You might have seen it, but I got hold of it! It's mine.'

'Wait,' said a third. 'We're ordinary men but this is no ordinary mango. We should take it to King Brahmadatta. This is a fruit fit for a king!'

The King had seen many wonders. But when he saw this mango – brought to him by courtiers on a velvet cushion while the rough fishermen waited outside, even he was astonished. He felt its smooth skin, like that of a baby. He sniffed its perfume and his eyes closed in pleasure.

'Cut me a slice,' he ordered. And when he tasted the flesh of the fruit, it was as if he had once tasted it in heaven and had been longing to taste it again ever since. But the fruit was large and King Brahmadatta was generous, so he gave some first to his queen, and then to his courtiers. They were all in raptures.

'We must find the tree that grew this fruit,' he said. 'Without delay!'

So, a large expedition set off, headed by Brahmadatta himself. They guessed that the fruit must have floated down the river, so they hunted the riverbanks on both sides for miles, high into the foothills of the Himalayas. After several days, those at the front of the expedition began to notice a beautiful perfume wafting to them on the evening breeze, and in a few minutes, they rounded a bend and came upon the tree. It was still heavy with mangoes, like hanging jewels. But to the King's horror, a swarm of monkeys were sitting in the great tree eating their way through its fruit. This was royal fruit – fit for a king, not a tribe of monkeys!

'Mount a guard!' ordered the King. It's getting dark now, but tomorrow, when it gets light, we'll kill every last monkey. Then they'll never return to gorge on this heavenly fruit. Tell the archers to get ready. Make sure no monkeys escape.'

The monkeys on the branch above the King's head overheard his plan. Chattering with anxiety, they went and reported it to the Monkey King immediately and begged to know how they might escape.

The Monkey King sighed. 'This is just as I feared. Men want everything for themselves. Our plight is serious. On one side of us lies the river. On the other side, the nearest tree is too far for a monkey to reach in a single leap.' He thought for some time. At length he announced,

'My people, I am the biggest and strongest among you. Have no fear. I will save you.'

The next morning, just after the first blush of dawn spread across the eastern sky, the Monkey King went to the furthest branch overhanging the river. He summoned his strength and sprang, in a huge leap, right across the river to a tree on the far bank. He found a long vine and tied one end to the tree and the other to his ankle. Then he leapt back across the river. His hands stretched out for the nearest branch and just managed to grasp it. But the vine was now as taut as a bowstring. It was too short to allow him to climb back to safety in the fruit tree.

'There is only one solution,' he said to the anxious tribe. 'You must each run across my back one at a time and follow the vine rope to the other side, where you will be safe. Hurry!'

For hours the Monkey King hung in space over the river, while each of the 80,000 monkeys ran across his back to safety. King Brahmadatta, meanwhile had woken up and was watching in amazement.

'Hurry, hurry!' the Monkey King groaned to the very last monkey. 'I can't hold on much longer.' Just as the last monkey reached the safety of the far bank, the Monkey King's back gave way. He fell to the ground in a broken heap and was immediately surrounded by men. King Brahmadatta waved them away.

'Fetch water and soothing oils to bathe the body of this great king!' he ordered them. Kneeling beside the Monkey King, he said in wonder, 'Monkey as you are, you have sacrificed your strength and your life to save your people.'

With difficulty the Monkey King replied, 'A king is the father of his people. They put their trust in me and it was my duty to do all I could to protect them. My happiness is that they are safe and I can die in peace. Understand, great Brahmadatta, that it is love, not power, that makes a great king.'

King Brahmadatta always remembered the last words of the Monkey King. He ordered a temple to be built in his honour, and offerings of the sweet fruit to be laid on its altar. And he always tried to be as noble a king as the Monkey King, offering his own strength and life in the service of his people.

Name _____

Leaders

PHOTOCOPIABLE

RE/Citizenship 45

Who makes the rules? – Islam

TEACHERS' NOTES

> This chapter, based on the story 'Muhammad's Night of Power', is designed to be spread over two or three lessons. The story could be coupled with 'The Betrayal of Jesus' (Chapter 4); both are about someone seeking and receiving divine inspiration. It could also be paired with 'The Ten Plagues of Egypt' (Chapter 10), which explores trust in divine authority.

Themes
Trust, authority, laws, inspiration

Aims
- To make children consider how laws are made, how people become leaders of a community, and whether we should communicate what we believe to be right to others.

Citizenship scheme of work
- Unit 5 – Living in a diverse world
- Unit 8 – How do rules and laws affect me?
- Unit 11 – In the media – what's the news?

Resources
- The story 'Muhammad's Night of Power' (page 48)
- Copies of the photocopiable sheet on page 50

Background
The story in this chapter is based closely on the account given in the Qu'ran of its text being revealed to Muhammad by the Angel Gabriel. It is particularly significant as Islam, like Christianity, is based very much on the authority of a single book, and on the trust placed in that authority.

Whole class starter
- Encourage the children to discuss different types of rules. Get them to give you examples of different types and give a reason for each one. You could suggest:
  Classroom "You have to put your hand up to answer a question and not shout out."
  School "No running in the corridors."
  Football "Obey the referee's decisions."
  Every day "Ask before you borrow something." "Say 'please' and 'thank-you'."
  'Unwritten rules' "Don't tell tales."
  (A controversial one!)
  Traffic "Drive on the left."
  Crime "Do not steal." "Do not murder."

- Give each child a copy of page 50. For each picture ask what rule is being shown. Then ask who they think made the rules and why.

- Before reading 'Muhammad's Night of Power' with the children, tell them that Muhammad lived in the sixth century (more than 1,500 years ago) and that he is the prophet of Islam, believed by Muslims to be the direct messenger of God (Allah). Explain that Islamic law is based on the Qu'ran, the holy book of Islam, just as Christian and Jewish law are based on the Ten Commandments. Make it clear that the Qu'ran is not just a book of laws. Now read the story.

46 RE/Citizenship – Ages 9–11

Activities

❏ Discuss with the children why Muhammad went to the cave in the hills, what happened to him there and how they might react if the same thing happened to them.

❏ Working individually, the children should write a paragraph about times when they are alone, how these times are different from times spent with others, and how these times alone can be valuable. You could give them the following sentence starters:
'When I am alone I think…'
'Being alone is different from being with other people because…'
'The good thing about being alone sometimes is that…'

❏ Remind children that Muhammad does not know what to make of his experience at first, but he takes it on trust that he has been spoken to by God (Allah). In teaching to others what the Angel Gabriel has told him (the contents of the Qu'ran), he is trusting in the authority of God. Ask the children to rank the following according to how far they can be trusted, firstly as sources of information and then as guides to how we should behave: you; headteacher; parents; grandparents; older brother or sister; friends; the Internet; newspapers; television; a religious leader; a police officer.

❏ Tell the children that in a democracy, such as this country, laws are voted for by elected Members of Parliament (MPs). Simulate this process by dividing the class into 'constituencies' (groups of four), each of which must elect one 'MP'. The MPs then go on to vote on a controversial issue relevant to your school – perhaps a new rule that older children are allowed to go in front of younger ones in the school dinner queue. You could introduce the issue before the MPs are voted in, so that the 'electorate' has a chance to consider the potential candidates' views.

Differentiation

❏ Give the children a shorter list to arrange in order in the trust and authority activity.

❏ For a more challenging activity, the children could list laws that they know exist in Britain (you could ask for a minimum of four). They could then write a paragraph explaining why each of these is a good thing, as well as giving any criticisms they have. They could also write about a law they think should be changed.

Extension

❏ Ask the children to make up their own 'big rules' like the Ten Commandments. They could start with ten and then try reducing them to five, three and, finally, one, making them more all-inclusive each time: for example, 'Love your neighbour as yourself' is a very inclusive rule, from which many more specific ones could spring.

❏ One of the 'big rules' in Islam is giving to the poor. The children could write about the merits (or otherwise) of this rule.

❏ Muhammad believes it is his duty to teach what he has learned. The children could discuss whether we all have a duty to tell other people how we think they should behave.

Plenary session

❏ Ask children to discuss what advice for living they might give their own grandchildren in the future. Possible topics for advice are:

• how to behave in school;

• how to choose friends;

• how to behave towards friends;

• what to do if threatened by others;

• what aims to have in life and how to achieve them.

RE/Citizenship – Ages 9–11   47

Muhammad's Night of Power

Once, in the great city of Mecca, in Arabia, there was a merchant called Muhammad. He worked hard at his business, buying, selling, discussing prices and making deals. But sometimes he liked to leave all this busy activity behind and walk off into the hills of Hira to think quietly and be alone. It seemed to him that in these peaceful hills, where he could make his heart as open as the hills themselves, God was closer to him. Muhammad was a thinker, a philosopher, a man who searched in himself for the meaning of life. In the hills, he would pray and think. Sometimes he would go without food for days to try to focus his thoughts on spiritual things. At other times, his wife Khadija would send a boy to take him food.

One year, when Muhammad was 39, he decided to go to the hills for the traditional time of religious fasting, now known as Ramadan. This was a time for going on a religious retreat. Muhammad left the bustle of the city and climbed up into the hills. This time he carried with him a bag of dates and barley to sustain him. He made his way to the cave where he had spent many hours praying and thinking in the past. The cave was dark, but it was also delightfully cool in the heat of the day. Moreover, there was little chance of Muhammad being disturbed there – or so he thought.

Muhammad prayed and meditated for many days. One night, just before dawn, as he was completely immersed in his meditations, he seemed to hear a voice. It seeped into his awareness, then grew louder and louder, seeming to fill the whole cave. It came from outside and inside Muhammad at the same time. It was not like any human voice.

Suddenly, a bright light filled the cave. Muhammad shielded his eyes, dazzled. When he dared to look up, there was an angel standing before him, holding out a cloth of green brocade. It had writing embroidered on it.

'Read!' commanded the angel.

Muhammad was amazed. 'I can't,' he said. Muhammad was clever, and a deep thinker, but as a merchant he had never really needed to learn to read.

A strange and frightening sensation gripped him. He was being squeezed by the angel.

Muhammad gasped as the angel released him and once again commanded: 'Read!'

'I cannot read,' said Muhammad more firmly. He did not enjoy the prospect of being squeezed again.

The angel looked at him sternly. There was no arguing with this angel. 'Read, in the name of your God, who created human beings from a drop of blood; in the name of Almighty

God, who taught human beings the use of the pen and what they did not know before.'

Seized by a strange power, Muhammad found himself doing what he had never done before. He read the verses that the angel held out, speaking them out loud. What is more, he carried on until he knew them perfectly, word for word.

As suddenly as the angel had arrived, Muhammad found himself alone, in a dark, silent cave in the mountains. He felt around him, still dazed. The cave seemed normal, though now the first hint of pale pink dawn was trickling in through the cave mouth. Muhammad got up and went outside. For him, it was the dawn of a new day in more ways than one! Although it would be hot later, the air was chilly now. Muhammad shivered and suddenly felt anxious. What was it that he had just experienced? Perhaps the cave was haunted by a spirit. Perhaps he had become ill without realising it. Without bothering to pick up his few belongings, he set off down the mountain.

Muhammad had gone only a short distance when he heard the huge voice again, roaring all around him: 'O Muhammad, you are the Messenger of God, and I am Gabriel.' Muhammad looked up and there was the figure of the angel, so big that it filled the whole horizon. Whichever way Muhammad looked, there it was. He tried to move, but he could go neither forward nor back until the angel had faded from view.

When Muhammad reached the outskirts of Mecca, the city was already awake. Women were fetching water. Men were driving goats through the streets. Merchants were hurrying off to make their deals. It was a normal day. As he came to his house, his wife Khadija came out to meet him.

'Husband,' she said, with concern in her voice, 'is something the matter?' Muhammad told her about his astonishing experience. It was wonderful but frightening. Was God punishing him? Khadija made him sit down quietly.

She reassured him, saying, 'You're a good man. You help orphans, the poor and the sick. You're honest in business. Surely God cannot be punishing you. Why don't you go to my cousin Waraqa and see what he thinks?'

Waraqa was a wise old man. He had been converted to Christianity and so, unlike most other Meccans, he already believed that there was only one God. When he heard Muhammad's tale he said, 'You have indeed been visited by the Angel Gabriel, God's messenger – as Moses once was. You should believe God's message. You must teach it to the world. But be prepared: not everyone will believe you.'

Eventually the message received by Muhammad was written down as the Qu'ran, the holy book of Islam. The beliefs of all Muslims are founded on this book.

Name _____

Rules and regulations

ACTIVITY SHEET 1

50 RE/Citizenship

PHOTOCOPIABLE

Respecting beliefs – Islam

TEACHERS' NOTES

> This chapter, based on the story 'The Cave, the Doves and the Spider' is designed to be spread over one or two lessons. The story could be coupled with 'The Betrayal of Jesus' (Chapter 4) – like Muhammad, Jesus is persecuted, though he responds differently. Alternatively, this story could be paired with 'The Ten Plagues of Egypt' (Chapter 10), which is also about a group escaping persecution through faith.

Themes
Religious persecution, trust in God, bravery, miracles

Citizenship scheme of work
- Unit 5 – Living in a diverse world
- Unit 8 – How do rules and laws affect me?
- Unit 11 – In the media – what's the news?

Aims
- To make children think about religious persecution and how to respond to it.

Resources
- The story 'The Cave, the doves and the Spider' (page 53)
- Copies of the writing frames (pages 55–57)

Background
The story in this chapter is from the Qu'ran, although it has been added to in popular Islamic literature. It shows Muhammad, before he was widely acknowledged as a prophet, showing faith in God, and that faith being rewarded by his being protected by nature. In a less specifically Muslim sense, the story could be seen as showing the wisdom of having a faith in the universe.

Whole class starter
- Ask the class if they know the meaning of the word 'persecute'. If no one does, explain that it means 'to harass, afflict, hunt down or put to death a group or an individual, especially for religious or political opinions'.
- Ask the class to suggest reasons for a group or individual being persecuted. Possible answers are: ethnic background, religious beliefs, political beliefs or just being different in some way.
- Explain that the story 'The Cave, the Doves and the Spider' is about Muhammad, the founder of Islam, and that in the story he is fleeing from persecution. Then read the story to the children.

Activities
- Lead a classroom discussion of the story. Points to consider:
  - Why did many Meccans find Muhammad a threat? (He preached that there was one God, and they worshipped many. The new religion also threatened to lose money for merchants depending on idol-worshipping pilgrims.)
  - Why did Muhammad not simply stand up to those who wished to assassinate him – and become a martyr if necessary? (We

RE/Citizenship – Ages 9–11 51

cannot be sure, but if he had died he might not have established the new religion.)

- Was Muhammad really helped by God (Allah) or just lucky? (And could being 'lucky' in some sense mean being helped by God, or the universe?)

❑ Ask children to retell the story in their own words, with the help of the writing frames on pages 55–57. They can choose to write from Ali's viewpoint, from Abu Bakr's viewpoint or from the viewpoint of one of the would-be assassins. Explain that they will have to try to put themselves in the shoes of the person telling the story – if they are a would-be assassin, they will have to include strong reasons for their wanting Muhammad dead.

❑ Encourage children to think about Ali and Abu Bakr's faith in Muhammad. They could write a dialogue in which one of these men explains their faith to a non-believer or an enemy of Muhammad.

Differentiation

❑ To make the writing frame activity easier, you could add more information or let the children tackle only part of the story. Alternatively, they could work in small groups, each child tackling just one prompt and writing one paragraph.

❑ For more challenge, don't give children a writing frame. You could limit this to the more able children in the class.

Extension

❑ The children could create a news story for the *Mecca Mail* reporting Muhammad's escape, including quotations from his followers. The report could be hostile to or supportive of Muhammad.

❑ The children could use the Internet to research and write about modern examples of religious persecution, particularly that of the Jews by the Nazis.

Plenary session

❑ Lead the class in a discussion of why some people persecute others. They could discuss in small groups and report to the class. Make a list or thought shower on the board of all the possible reasons. Encourage the children to realise that the persecutors may, at bottom, feel afraid or threatened by those whom they persecute.

The Cave, the Doves and the Spider

Muhammad is the Prophet of Islam, the religion of millions of people worldwide. But at one time, only a few people believed in his teachings and he was a hunted man.

About 10 years after Muhammad had begun to teach people that there was only one God (Allah), his uncle Abu Talib died. This uncle had always protected Muhammad from his enemies. And now, as Muhammad began to gather more followers, he also gathered more enemies. Many people in the city of Mecca did not like Muhammad's claim that there was only one God. They worshipped many gods, and bowed down to idols. Mecca was a place of pilgrimage for idol-worshippers, who travelled from far away to worship a great black stone in the centre of the city. These pilgrims spent money in the city, which lined the pockets of the shopkeepers and traders.

So, even though Muhammad had already planned to move away from Mecca to Medina, his enemies plotted to assassinate him. The plotters came from several tribes, or clans. No tribe wanted to be the only one guilty of killing Muhammad, so they agreed that one man from each tribe would join an assassination squad. The squad would lie in wait for Muhammad and murder him.

The murderers had not reckoned on Muhammad having help from Allah. The night before the planned assassination, the Angel Gabriel came to Muhammad and told him, 'Do not sleep in your own bed tonight.' Muhammad guessed why, and told his faithful follower Ali to take his place in his bed that night and wrap himself in Muhammad's blanket. 'You will be perfectly safe,' said Muhammad, and this was good enough for Ali, who was quite willing to die for the Prophet if necessary.

Under cover of darkness, the assassins gathered outside the house waiting for Muhammad to emerge. When Muhammad did come out, he took up a handful of dust and threw it over the men's heads, reciting some verses from the Qu'ran. With the help of Allah, this temporarily blinded them and Muhammad and his servant Abu Bakr were able to pass by completely unnoticed.

They set off, heading for the cave of Thawr in the mountains, about five miles from Mecca. They planned to hide here until it was safe for them to carry on to Medina.

In the morning, the would-be assassins were furious when only Ali came out of Muhammad's house and they realised that they had been tricked. They sent out a search party to hunt for Muhammad. They had a pretty good idea that he would be somewhere in the mountains.

After searching for three days, the pursuers came to the cave where Muhammad and Abu Bakr were hiding. They got down from their camels to look inside the cave. Abu Bakr was afraid and felt sure that now they would be caught, but Muhammad trusted in Allah and quietly reassured him.

What Abu Bakr did not realise was that Allah had sent them some helpers. A pair of doves had built their nest in the entrance to the cave and the female bird was sitting quietly on her eggs. The pursuers saw this and thought it unlikely that anyone could be inside the cave. When they saw a spider's web stretched unbroken across the narrow entrance, they were sure that Muhammad could not possibly be hiding here.

One of them spat into the dust.

'Come on,' he sighed. 'We're wasting our time here.' So the men urged on their camels and went to look elsewhere. With the help of Allah, two doves and a spider, Muhammad and Abu Bakr had escaped.

Ali

ACTIVITY SHEET 1

Write about Ali's reaction and feelings, then about the night he spends in the house.
When Muhammad asked me to sleep in his bed instead of him, wrapped in his blanket, I immediately…

Write about the reaction of the men to Ali, and his reaction to them.
In the morning, I got up, got dressed, and left the house. It was surrounded by armed men…

Write about what Ali hears of Muhammad's escape and how he feels about that.
Later I heard…

PHOTOCOPIABLE

RE/Citizenship 55

Abu Bakr

ACTIVITY SHEET 2

Write about their journey to the cave.
I was so happy to be travelling with my master Muhammad to a new life in Medina…

Write about what it was like in the cave.
That night we came to a cave. It was…

Write about how Abu Baker felt, how Muhammad reassured him, and what happened in the end.
When we heard the snorting of camels and the sound of voices outside the cave, I felt…

Assassin

Give the reasons for Muhammad's enemies wanting him dead.
None of us wanted to be the one to kill Muhammad. Even so, someone had to, because…

Write about how Muhammad threw dust and temporarily blinded the men waiting for him.
Something strange happened to us. It was as if…

Write about Ali coming out and how the assassin felt about that.
We waited all night. The next morning a man came out of the house. It was…

Tell the rest of the escape story. Will the man be angry or pleased that he didn't have to kill Muhammad?
Later, I heard that…

CHAPTER 9

Deciding what to do – Jainism

TEACHERS' NOTES

This chapter, based on the Jain story of 'King Hansa' is designed to last for one or two lessons. The story could be linked to 'Lakshmi and the Wise Washerwoman' (Chapter 5), which also involved devotion and virtue, or to 'David and Goliath' (Chapter 11) or 'The Five Beloved Ones' (Chapter 13), both of which involve courage – albeit a different kind of courage from that exhibited by King Hansa.

Themes

Honesty, non-violence

Citizenship scheme of work

- Unit 2 – Choices
- Unit 4 – People who help us
- Unit 8 – How do rules and laws affect me?

Aims

To make children consider:
- whether it is always possible to avoid telling lies;
- whether non-violence is always the right policy;
- how we should respond to dishonest or violent people.

Resources

- The story 'King Hansa' (page 60)
- Copies of the photocopiable sheet on page 63

Background

Jainism is less well known than, say, Christianity or Islam. However, there are 3.2 million Jains in India and between 25,000 and 30,000 in the UK (mostly in Leicester and London). A central principle of Jainism is its concern for the welfare of all living beings. Hence all Jains are vegetarian and very strict Jains will even sweep the path before them to avoid treading on insects. Correct conduct is vital in Jainism, and the most important aspect of this is ahimsa – non-violence (also a principle of Hinduism). Another aspect of correct conduct is strict truthfulness. King Hansa, in the story featured in this chapter, manages to avoid causing harm to living beings, but also avoids telling lies.

Whole class starter

❑ Ask the children if they think it is always right to tell the truth. Prompt a short class discussion with these questions:

- How do you feel when you tell a lie?
- How do others feel when they find you have lied? What do they think of you?
- Would you ever tell a lie to protect someone else?

❑ Now read the story. At certain points in the text there are prompts suggesting that you pause and ask the class what King Hansa should do or say.

Activities

❑ Hand out copies of page 63. Ask the children to mark each statement on the sheet according to how far they agree with it.

❑ Organise a hot-seating activity. In groups, the children take it in turns to take on the roles of characters in the story (or just King Hansa). Other children then ask them questions about why they acted in the way they did. Those in the 'hot seat' have to answer in character.

❑ Identify the four situations in which King Hansa makes a choice. Ask the children to list all the other options the King had in each situation.

Differentiation

❑ For more challenge, ask the children to give written explanations for their choices on the activity sheet. For less challenge, limit the number of situations for which children must list King Hansa's options.

Extension

❑ The children could use books and the Internet to find out more about the principles of Jainism, especially not harming living creatures.

❑ The children could write a story in which someone has to choose between violence and non-violence, for example in self defence against bullies.

❑ The children could read about Mahatma Ghandi. He was a Hindu not a Jain, but championed non-violent resistance to injustice.

Plenary session

❑ Ask children to consider whether it is possible for them to live without ever doing harm to other living beings and without ever being dishonest in any way. If they conclude that it is not possible (for example they may feel that they have to eat meat), ask if these aims are nonetheless worthwhile.

King Hansa

In the city of Rajpur, there was once a good king named Hansa. He was known for his honesty and for his belief that it was never right to use violence.

Some distance from Rajpur, on top of a high mountain, there stood a beautiful temple. During one month of the year, at full moon, people came from far away to visit and worship in this temple. King Hansa had decided that this year he would visit the temple, so he summoned his ministers.

'Ministers, I am going on a pilgrimage. I am leaving you in charge of the kingdom. Rule my people with justice and wisdom.'

The ministers were uneasy about this, and it turned out that they were right to be. A few days after King Hansa had departed with his companions and servants, a neighbouring king, Arjuna, attacked the city with his army.

Despite a fierce fight, King Hansa's army was defeated and Arjuna took charge of the kingdom.

When news of this reached King Hansa and his companions, they urged him to return and challenge Arjuna.

'What would you do if you were the king?'

The King was determined.

'We are on a spiritual mission,' he insisted. 'We should carry on to the temple. When we get there, we can pray for the safety of my people.'

King Hansa's companions and servants were unhappy about this course of action. They muttered among themselves: 'Has he gone mad?' 'He's not in the real world!' 'Even a king has responsibilities!' One by one they slunk away.

After a few more days, King Hansa found himself accompanied by just one man – his umbrella-carrier. King Hansa gave the umbrella-carrier his royal clothes and jewels to carry – and soon afterwards he disappeared. King Hansa did not know if the man had deserted him or simply became lost in the forest, but he did know that now he was alone, with no protection.

Still determined, the King was trudging on up the forest path when a deer dashed across his path, big-eyed and panting. A few moments later a hunter appeared in pursuit, carrying a bow.

'Did you see a deer?' demanded the hunter.

'What would you do if you were the king?'

King Hansa knew that if he helped the hunter, the deer would probably die. But nor did he want to tell a lie. So, instead, he said, 'I come from Rajpur.'

'Indeed. But which way did my deer go?'

'I am King Hansa.'

'Maybe so, but you're no use to me!' said the hunter angrily as he plunged off into the forest.

The King was tired now, so he sat down under a tree to rest. While he sat, some armed robbers came by, talking about their plan to rob a group of monks on their way to the temple on the mountain. The robbers failed to notice King Hansa. While the King was wondering what to do about this, a group of police officers appeared on the path. The robbers quickly hid in the bushes before they could be seen.

'Did you see some suspicious looking characters come by here a little while ago?' they asked. 'We're tracking some robbers who may be planning to rob the monks on their way to the temple. We have orders to kill them if necessary, to protect the monks.'

Again, King Hansa had a tough decision.

'What would you do if you were the king?'

If he revealed the hiding place of the robbers, they would very likely be killed. If he did not, the monks might well be harmed instead. He thought to himself, 'Truth is supposed to protect people, not harm them.' With this thought in his mind, he addressed the police officers: 'My friends, your job is to protect the monks. Why not find the monks and guard them? If the robbers attack, you can fend them off. But perhaps when they see such a guard, they will just give up and go home!'

The police officers liked this idea, and went off to find the monks. The robbers, realising that the King had deliberately protected them, offered him their services.

'I have no need of your service,' he said. 'If you wish to repay me, simply give up your life of crime and become good citizens instead.'

'He's right, you know,' said the robber chief to the rest. And they all turned over a new leaf and became honest men.

Shortly after this, King Hansa heard the sound of hooves. Soon a group of soldiers appeared on horseback. 'Hey you! Have you seen King Hansa?'

'What do you want with him?' asked the King calmly.

'We're the new king's men. We've been sent to catch and kill King Hansa,' said their captain.

'What would you do if you were the king?'

Honest as ever, King Hansa stepped forward. 'I am King Hansa,' he announced. 'If your orders are to kill me, then that's what you must do.' Then he closed his eyes in meditation and waited calmly for death.

At that moment a flash of light hit the forest and an angel appeared. The soldiers' horses reared up and then galloped away. As King Hansa shielded his eyes, the angel spoke: 'I am so impressed by your honesty and kindness that I have captured Arjuna and returned your kingdom to the care of your trusted ministers. My chariot awaits to take you to the temple.'

King Hansa arrived at the temple on the mountaintop in the golden chariot. When he had worshipped there the angel returned him to his kingdom. King Hansa forgave and released Arjuna and his men, congratulated his own ministers, and once again took control of his kingdom. King Hansa's people were happy and he continued to rule them wisely and justly for many years to come.

Name _____

The King's choices

Task 1

Read these statements. Circle one box for each to show how far you agree.

1. King Hansa should have stayed to protect his people, not gone off to visit the temple.

    | Agree | Disagree | Not sure |

2. King Hansa should have been more helpful to the hunter.

    | Agree | Disagree | Not sure |

3. If King Hansa really wanted to protect the deer, he should have sent the hunter in the wrong direction.

    | Agree | Disagree | Not sure |

4. King Hansa should have told the police officers where the thieves were hiding.

    | Agree | Disagree | Not sure |

5. King Hansa didn't need to tell the soldiers who he was and risk being killed.

    | Agree | Disagree | Not sure |

Task 2

Imagine that you are King Hansa.
Explain why you acted as you did on each of these occasions:

I went on a pilgrimage to the temple because...

I did not help or mislead the hunter because...

I did not tell the police officers where the thieves were because...

I told the soldiers I was King Hansa because...

CHAPTER 10

Rights and promises – Judaism

TEACHERS' NOTES

> This chapter should be spread over two or three lessons. The story, 'The Ten Plagues of Egypt', is a relatively long one, and has been divided into two parts. The story raises many issues, including human rights, promises, and the use of force (in this case, supplied by divine intervention) to retaliate against an oppressor. It could be linked to 'Muhammad's Night of Power' or 'The Betrayal of Jesus', which both involve trust in divine authority. It could also be linked to 'Monster-Slayer and Born-of-Water Visit Their Father'.

Themes

Human rights, persistence, promises, divine deliverance

Citizenship scheme of work

- Unit 2 – Choices
- Unit 7 – Children's rights – human rights
- Unit 8 – How do rules and laws affect me?

Aims

To make children consider:
- what is meant by the concept of 'human rights' and how this relates to 'children's rights';
- issues surrounding resistance to oppression;
- how people reach group decisions.

Resources

- The story 'The Ten Plagues of Egypt' (page 66)
- Copies of the photocopiable sheets on pages 72 and 73

Background

The story of 'The Ten Plagues of Egypt' is taken from the Old Testament. If necessary, explain that this consists of a collection of writings dating from before the birth of Jesus. The New Testament was all written after the birth of Jesus (from which the start of our calendar is taken). The story is important in Jewish faith because it shows the one God enabling the faithful Jews to triumph over the Egyptians – who worshipped many gods. It also underlines the concept of the Jews as a people 'chosen' by God. The distinction is symbolised by the marking of Jewish doors, so that the Angel of Death passes them by. This event is still celebrated in the Jewish Feast of the Passover.

Whole class starter

❏ Lead the class in a short brainstorming session on what they understand by the word 'freedom'. You will probably get answers such as: not being in prison, being able to do whatever you want or not having to obey rules. Explain that if people are to live together no one can have total freedom to do what they want, but that in many societies people agree on 'human rights' – basic freedoms that everyone is entitled to.

❏ Divide the class into small groups and give each group a copy of page 72. Ask the groups to do one of the following activities:

- discuss why each of these rights is important and see if they can agree which is the most important;
- choose one of the rights and talk about why it is important, and be prepared to explain to the class why it is important.

64 RE/Citizenship – Ages 9–11

❏ Before reading the story 'The Ten Plagues of Egypt', tell children that it is from the Old Testament of the Bible and is probably based on real events. Explain that the Israelites, the ancestors of the Jews, were slaves in Egypt for centuries and may have helped to build the pyramids in which pharaohs were buried. You could add that at that time many societies thought slavery was acceptable. Say that there is far less slavery now, but that it still exists illegally in some parts of the world. It became illegal in Niger (not to be confused with Nigeria) only in 2004.

❏ Now read the first part of the story (or perhaps the whole story if you have an attentive Year 6 class). Before starting on the second half in another session, remind children of what has happened up to that point. You could see if they can remember what plagues have taken place so far – water into blood, frogs, gnats, flies, cattle sickness, boils.

Activities

After reading the first half of the story, choose from the following activities. In a subsequent lesson, read the second half of the story and choose further activities.

❏ The children could act out scenes from the story. The opening scene would be a good one to act out. They will also enjoy acting out scenes based on the various plagues, particularly the frogs. A re-enactment of the final pursuit across the Red Sea would have to be done with a lot of imagination! Several scenes could be staged in sequence during a school assembly.

❏ Ask the children to write a letter to the Pharaoh arguing the case for the Israelites to be set free. The letter could be from either an Egyptian who might be symathetic or an Israelite.

❏ The children could write a diary for the Pharaoh, reflecting his attitude towards the Israelites and some of his changes of heart.

❏ Ask the children to find Egypt and the Red Sea in an atlas and to draw their own map showing the route of the Exodus.

❏ Ask the children to illustrate scenes from the story. You could coordinate this to produce a frieze with brief captions. These should indicate what the Israelites wanted and why.

❏ Give the children copies of page 73, 'Rights for children'. Ask them to decide which of the selected rights were probably denied to Israelite children.

Differentiation

❏ Children who find it difficult to write the letter could be given a writing frame:
Dear Pharaoh, I think the Israelites should be set free because …
• *Reason 1*
• *Reason 2*
• *Reason 3*
If you set them free, this would be a good thing for you because…
people would think you were…
or
you would not have to put up with …
Your humble servant…

❏ A more challenging task would be for children to explore the phrase in the selected children's rights, 'unless this breaks the rights of others'. They could think about how one person's right to do something could interfere with someone else's.

Extension

❏ Children could design a poster for children's rights.

❏ They could research children's rights on the Internet, beginning with the simplified version of the Convention on the Rights of the Child, to be found at:
www.savethechildren.org.uk/eyetoeye/teachers/secondary/resources/uncrc.htm

Plenary session

❏ See if children can now name some of the rights that they enjoy, and which were probably not enjoyed by Israelite children.

RE/Citizenship – Ages 9–11   65

The Ten Plagues of Egypt

Part 1

Moses and his brother Aaron stood before Pharaoh, who addressed the brothers in a loud voice: 'Prove yourselves by working a miracle. And I haven't got all day!' He waited. His courtiers exchanged glances. Some were amused, but others had heard that this man Moses and his brother had special powers and weren't bluffing when they said their God would free the Israelites from Egyptian slavery.

Moses spoke quietly to Aaron, who immediately flung his rod down onto the marble floor of the palace. There was a gasp of shock as the Egyptians retreated from the writhing snake that appeared in place of Aaron's rod.

Pharaoh was not very impressed. 'Not bad,' he said. 'Magicians – show our Israelite guests that they're not the only ones with tricks up their sleeves!' At this, twelve magicians stepped up and threw down their rods. At once, twelve more snakes reared up from the floor, tongues flickering towards the fearful crowd. Pharaoh smiled triumphantly. But the smile was wiped from his face when the snake that had sprung from Aaron's rod swallowed each of the others in turn, before turning back into a rod. 'Get out!' shouted Pharaoh at Moses and Aaron.

'Well – that didn't work, did it?' said Aaron to Moses as they left the palace. 'Pharaoh still didn't give us what we want. It's not so much to ask – permission for our people to go into the desert for three days and make sacrifices to God.'

'Aaron,' said Moses, 'God warned us that Pharaoh wouldn't give in easily. The Israelites have been the slaves of Egypt for centuries. How else would Pharaoh get his pyramids built? Don't worry. The Lord will make him give in.'

Sure enough, God soon spoke to Moses and told him to warn Pharaoh that the River Nile would be turned into blood if he didn't let the Israelites go and worship. Moses went to Pharaoh as he was going to the river to bathe. 'Pharaoh, you see this water you wash in? My God warns that if you don't let us go, he will turn every drop to blood.'

Pharaoh was not too worried. How could a couple of rebel Israelites turn a river into blood? The next day he found himself drinking wine with his breakfast instead of water. Few of his people had this luxury:

that morning they had found, to their horror, that the water they usually took from the river had turned to blood. They had to dig deep holes in their yards, in the hope of finding a little muddy water at the bottom. But even this failed to impress Pharaoh.

Seven days later, Moses and Aaron returned, with new instructions from God. 'Pharaoh,' began Moses, 'if you don't let us go, our God will send a plague of frogs.'

Pharaoh thought that frogs didn't sound too bad – and, anyway, his own magicians could pull frogs out of a hat for a party trick!

But Pharaoh wasn't amused the next day. Frogs hopped and crawled out of the Nile in their thousands. The croaking was deafening. They leaped through open windows into people's food, even into their ovens. Pharaoh had his servants sweep the frogs from his private chamber, but when they pulled back his sheet at bedtime, more frogs leaped into view.

'That does it!' said Pharaoh.

Next day, he promised Moses and Aaron that their people could go and worship. 'Just get rid of the frogs!' he said. Aaron waved his rod and the frogs were all killed, but the Egyptians still had piles of dead frogs to deal with. The smell was terrible.

But Pharaoh hardened his heart and decided to refuse them, and so another plague came. This time it was gnats – irritating little insects that buzz in your hair and bite, and suck your blood. Where the Egyptians lived, the air was thick with them. Around the Israelites' homes there were none. And even Pharaoh's magicians weren't able to get rid of the gnats.

'This must truly be the work of God,' Pharaoh bitterly admitted and again agreed to let the Israelites go into the desert, but all too soon, his heart hardened and he went back on his word. He soon had cause to regret this; the next plague was one of flies. Again, they avoided the Israelites, but throughout the rest of Egypt they swarmed like a buzzing, crawling blanket. They covered the Egyptians' food, filled their hair and even got into their mouths when they spoke. They laid eggs which hatched into maggots, which soon became more flies.

PHOTOCOPIABLE

'All right,' said the exhausted Pharaoh to Moses and Aaron. 'Go and sacrifice to your God – but do it within the land of Egypt.'

'But Pharaoh,' protested Moses, 'if we make our sacrifices within your land, your people will be offended and stone us. We must go three days' journey into the desert.'

'Oh, all right then – but just don't go too far away. And get rid of the flies!'

As soon as the flies were gone, Pharaoh once again hardened his heart and forbade the Israelites to leave. Moses and Aaron came before him again. This time they threatened him with a plague on all Egyptian cattle, horses, sheep, donkeys and camels. Nothing with hooves would be spared, unless it belonged to the Israelites.

Pharaoh still would not budge, and his people's animals died. There was no milk or meat, no donkeys to work, no camels to ride. Life for the Egyptians became harder every day and still Pharaoh would not give in. So Moses, following God's instructions, made every Egyptian break out in large painful boils.

Even now, Pharaoh would not allow the Israelites to go. When Moses and Aaron returned to his palace, instead of sitting on his throne to receive them he was standing up and looking very uncomfortable, and he had ugly lumps on his face.

'So far, you've got off lightly,' warned Moses. 'Now this is going to get serious. My God says that unless you do as we ask, there's going to be a hailstorm like nothing you've ever seen before.'

Part 2

When word got round that there was going to be a huge hailstorm, those of Pharaoh's servants who believed in Moses's God took their families, and any animals they had left, into their homes and waited. When the storm broke, it was every bit as bad as Moses had promised. Fire and lightning flashed in the heavens, crops were ruined, trees flattened. Hailstones the size of coconuts pelted through flimsy straw roofs and killed people and animals out in the open. The storm avoided the Israelites, of course.

'All right, all right! I know I've sinned. Ask your Lord to stop this infernal storm and you can go!' Pharaoh looked tired, and his personal doctor was dabbing ointment on an egg-sized swelling on his head.

Moses left the city and stretched his hands out to the Lord. The storm stopped. It was strangely quiet. The sun came out and the deserted streets began to steam. 'Perhaps now Pharaoh will have learned his lesson,' said Aaron to his brother.

But soon after this the brothers had word that Pharaoh had changed his mind again, and they were back at the royal palace, this time threatening him with a plague of locusts – insects like large grasshoppers that travel in swarms and eat anything that grows.

The Egyptians pleaded with Pharaoh: 'We're being ruined. Please, Great One, give them what they want.'

So Pharaoh summoned Moses and Aaron and said, 'You may go if you leave your children behind.'

'No,' said Moses. 'We must all go – with our children, and all our animals.'

'I don't trust you,' complained Pharaoh. 'Your men can go – no one else. Now get out of my sight!'

Moses would not accept half measures. He stretched his rod over the land, and an east wind sprang up and blew all night. It brought with it clouds of locusts, which ate what was left of the crops. Every leaf on every tree was eaten, and every last ear of corn. Those who had no grain stores now began to starve. Famine gripped the land.

'Forgive me,' pleaded Pharaoh to Moses. His pride, at last, seemed broken. 'I have sinned. Please ask your God to save my people.'

So Moses drove the locusts that had been plaguing Egypt into the Red Sea. But once again, despite everything, Pharaoh broke his promise. This time, God blotted out the sun so that the Egyptians were cast into darkness for three days on end. The Israelites had light, but the Egyptians could not even see their hands in front of their faces.

'Ow! That really does it!' fumed Pharaoh, as he banged into another door. 'Somebody fetch Moses!'

This time Pharaoh offered a little more: 'You can go if you leave your cattle behind,' he announced.

'Sorry, no. They come too,' Moses insisted.

'Then get out of my sight!' shouted Pharaoh. 'If you ever see my face again, you're dead!'

Then God promised Moses he would bring down one last plague on the Egyptians – the worst one of all. This was the death of the first born.

Each Israelite family had to take a lamb, wait until the middle of the month, and then slaughter it. They were to smear some of its blood on their doorposts and then roast the lamb and eat it. All of the Israelites did as they were told.

The blood smeared on the doorposts was a sign. Wherever the Angel of Death saw it, he passed over it, leaving the family unharmed. But in every Egyptian family, the first born – the eldest child – was killed by the Angel of Death. It happened just after midnight. Throughout Egypt, a great wailing began, as people discovered their dead children.

So, finally, Pharaoh gave in and allowed the Israelites – men, women, children and all their cattle – to leave Egypt. After 430 years of slavery, the Israelites packed up their belongings, herded together their cattle, and began the great journey out of Egypt – the Exodus.

By the time the last of the million or more Israelites had disappeared beyond the borders of Egypt, Pharaoh was already having second thoughts. 'What have I done?' he asked himself. 'Who will do all the work now?' He paced up and down shouting irritably at advisers who offered him advice.

Finally, he banged his fist down on a marble table-top as hard as his heart had now become. 'Equip my chariots. We will pursue these Israelites!'

The mighty Egyptian army drew close to the Israelites as they camped by the Red Sea, on the edge of the desert. The people of Israel saw the dust raised by the Egyptian chariots, like a storm on the horizon. Some of them cried out bitterly to Moses, 'Did you bring us out here to die because there were no graves in Egypt?' But Moses told them to have faith.

Sure enough, God made a huge cloud roll up to hide them from the Egyptians all through the night. In the morning, acting as always on God's orders, Moses waved his rod over the Red Sea. His people waited tensely to see what would happen. Then they pulled their cloaks around them as a strong east wind began to blow. After a short time, to their amazement, they saw that the wind was piling up the waves to make a broad, dry road between them. The waves crashed and sucked at the sand, but before long they stood towering in two huge, quivering walls on either side. And with another wave of his staff, Moses led his people on, between the walls of water.

The heavily armed Egyptian chariots set off in pursuit, but they sank up to their axles in the mud. Terrified horses reared up before the threatening waves and broke their harnesses. But worse was to come. Moses turned to face his pursuers and waved his rod one last time. The walls of water came crashing down and drowned the Egyptian army. Meanwhile the Israelites marched on to safety across the dry seabed. As they passed, the walls of water drew like curtains behind them, and as they finally came to the far shore, the sea roared back into its usual place.

On the far shore, the Israelites looked back in relief, and Miriam, the sister of Moses and Aaron, took a tambourine and burst into song to lead a victory dance. God had delivered them from the Egyptians. They were free at last!

Our rights

freedom to work and earn a living

freedom of speech

freedom to travel within one's own country

justice within the law

freedom to practise one's religion

freedom from slavery

72 RE/Citizenship

PHOTOCOPIABLE

Rights for children

These are some of the rights listed in the United Nations Convention on the Rights of the Child.

Article 9   You have the right to live with your parents, unless it is bad for you.

Article 10 If you and your parents are living in separate countries, you have the right to get back together and live in the same place.

Article 11 You should not be kidnapped.

Article 12 You have the right to an opinion and for it to be listened to and taken seriously.

Article 13 You have the right to find out things and say what you think, through making art, speaking and writing, unless it breaks the rights of others.

Article 14 You have the right to think what you like and practise whatever religion you want, with your parents' guidance.

Article 15 You have the right to be with friends and join or set up clubs, unless this breaks the rights of others.

Article 16 You have the right to a private life. For instance, you can keep a diary that other people are not allowed to see.

Article 19 You have the right to be protected from being hurt or badly treated.

Article 27 You have the right to a good enough standard of living. This means you should have food, clothes and a place to live.

Article 28 You have the right to education.

CHAPTER 11

Could you be a hero? – Judaism

TEACHERS' NOTES

> This chapter is designed to work over one or two lessons. The story of 'David and Goliath', upon which it is based, could be coupled with 'The Five Beloved Ones (Chapter 13) or 'The Cave, the Doves and the Spider' (Chapter 8), both of which also involve trust in God.

Themes
Courage, risk taking, contributing to the community

Citizenship scheme of work
- Unit 1 – Taking part
- Unit 2 – Choices
- Unit 11 – In the media – what's the news?

Aims
- To make children think about what they might achieve in life, even against seemingly difficult odds, and how their achievement might contribute to society.

Resources
- The story 'David and Goliath' (page 76)
- Copies of the photocopiable sheets on pages 80 and 81 (differentiated)

Background
The story of 'David and Goliath' is taken from the Old Testament. (See Chapter 10 'Background' for explanation of Old Testament.) David is significant in Jewish faith as a hero and as an ancestor of Jesus, viewed by many Jews as a prophet (but not as the Messiah or Son of God). Judaism emphasises the importance of being part of the community, and David does a great service to his community by killing Goliath. He continues to be an inspiration to many Jews.

Whole class starter
❑ Ask the children what they understand by 'being a hero'. If they focus on conventional ideas of heroism or 'not crying when you hurt yourself', try to expand their understanding by suggesting other types of heroism:

- remaining positive in times of trouble or illness;
- being honest when we could get out of trouble by keeping silent;
- saying and doing what we believe in, even if it could make us unpopular;
- resisting peer pressure;
- risking losing face by attempting a challenge.

❑ Ask the children to think of a time when they have been brave. If they are reluctant, you could suggest they think of someone they know who has been brave. They could then list different types of bravery.

❑ Finally, get them to list people in their community who are heroic in some way – doing brave things that benefit the community. Obvious examples are the police and fire brigade, but you could add:

- nurses and doctors;
- community leaders who sometimes have to make unpopular decisions;
- the army (not usually 'in the community' but acting on the community's behalf).

You could also ask them if they think teachers have to be brave.

❑ Before reading the story 'David and Goliath' tell the children that it is from the Old Testament of the Bible. Now read the story.

Activities

❑ Give each child a copy of page 80 and ask them to answer the questions, to test their understanding of the story.

❑ The children could act out the response to the news of David's victory, emphasising his bravery and what it means for all concerned.

❑ The children could write a story called 'A modern day David and Goliath', in which a child stands up to someone apparently stronger, and wins – to the benefit of others. This could easily be related to bullying. Emphasise that 'standing up' to someone does not have to mean physically fighting them.

Differentiation

❑ For an easier comprehension, give children a copy of page 81, which has similar questions but gives multiple choice options for the answers.

❑ For a more challenging activity, the children could write a short essay explaining why and how David was such a hero – what was the challenge, what inspired him, and how this benefited the Israelites.

Extension

❑ The children could write a letter from David to his mother giving his version of the story.

❑ The children could act out part of the story; for example, David announcing to Saul that he intends to fight Goliath.

❑ Ask the children to tell the story from the Philistine point of view – perhaps in a news story for the 'Philistine Herald'.

Plenary session

❑ Encourage all the children to think of, and tell the class, something that they would like to do for the benefit of the community, whether now or when they grow up.

RE/Citizenship – Ages 9–11

David and Goliath

This is a story about how my brother David became famous overnight. He was the youngest of our father's eight sons. Only a boy really. That's why he wasn't in the army. My eldest brother, Eliab, joined first.

'I'm off to serve my king – the mighty Saul,' he said proudly as he left the house. 'It's goodbye sleepy little Bethlehem, hello fame and fortune!'

We watched him go, with a mixture of envy and relief that it wasn't us.

Next it was the turn of Abinadab. 'You next, Shammah,' he said to me, punching me playfully on the shoulder.

Our Israelite army was hard pressed by the Philistines, and King Saul wanted to swell the ranks with more soldiers. Before long, it was my turn. My father held me by the shoulders. 'Shammah, make me proud!' he said. I told him I'd try. Mind you, by then I was wondering if the chance would ever come.

Sure enough, the camp was as I expected. There was tension, and men keyed up ready to fight, but no battle. The reason was this. The Philistines, our sworn enemies, had put forward a champion. His name was Goliath.

Now, this Goliath wasn't just a run-of-the-mill sort of a champion who'd won a few fights and fancied his chances. He was a monster of a man, practically a giant. When he came down into the valley that separated the two armies, we all got a clear view of him. He wasn't just big; he was colossal. Even at that distance we could see the sun glinting on his great bronze helmet, his chain mail and his bronze shin-guards. The man who held Goliath's shield looked like a dwarf beside him.

The other men knew pretty much what to expect next, because this stalemate had gone on for weeks now. Every day, Goliath came down and challenged our army to find a man to fight him, but no one ever would. And I can tell you, King Saul was getting pretty fed up with this. Someone was going to have to volunteer soon – or else!

Goliath's voice roared up to us on our hill like thunder: 'Puny little Israelites,' he began (politely, by his standards), 'Why do you stand there trembling like little girls? Send a man to fight me. If he kills me, the Philistines will be your servants forever. But if I win, you will be ours. I defy the might of Israel! Send me a man to fight – if you dare!'

On the opposite hill, the Philistine army cheered happily, as well they might. Our army was silent, apart from a few mutters. 'Well?' demanded King Saul. 'Is there no one with the courage to fight for the glory of Israel?' My brother Eliab, always a show-off, started to raise his hand, but as Saul glanced round, he pretended that he'd only meant to scratch the back of his head.

'Well, don't all shout at once!' snorted Saul. 'Call yourselves an army? Pathetic!'

Abinadab leaned over to me while keeping his eyes fixed on Saul. 'Oh-oh – I sense a black mood coming on…' Our great king was not an easy man to serve. He was known for his moods. He'd just get really depressed and gloomy and start shouting for people to be sent to prison.

Now, this is where our youngest, David, comes in. Because he was the youngest, our mother had mollycoddled him. She wanted him to find a job in the palace, not just be a rough-tough soldier like his older brothers. She'd persuaded our father, Jesse, to pay for him to have harp lessons. I ask you! To be fair, David was also very good with sheep, and he did a great job of looking after our flocks. Even played them a few tunes to help them get to sleep! But seriously, he could really play that harp. So, when Saul's servants decided that some soothing sounds might cheer Saul up, they sent for David.

Our little brother became a big hit at once. He played his harp to soothe Saul when he had one of his moods, and he became Saul's shield carrier too. What with all that, and looking after the sheep, David really had his hands full. Even so, when our father told him to take us some loaves of bread and some grain, and some cheese for our commander, he managed to find someone to look after the sheep and set off to the camp.

David arrived just in time for Goliath's usual challenge. By now, our men were trying to ignore Goliath in the hope that he'd just go away. But David seemed astonished by this.

'Who is this Philistine who dares to insult our army, our nation, and the living God?'

PHOTOCOPIABLE

RE/Citizenship 77

He paused, then added, 'How shall the man who kills him be rewarded?'

This caused a bit of a stir. One man looked hard at David. 'The king will give him great riches, and his own daughter's hand in marriage. His whole family shall be honoured.'

Eliab, probably worried about being shamed by his own baby brother, pushed David and shouted at him: 'What are you even doing here? Who's looking after the sheep? You've just skived off to get a look at the battle!'

But David stood his ground. 'I'm going to find Saul,' he retorted. I followed him, worried that he'd do something silly. I was right – he did. When he got to Saul's tent, he asked to see him. He was a favourite with Saul, so the king invited him in and I followed behind.

'My lord,' said David to Saul. 'I am your servant, and I will fight Goliath.'

To Saul's credit, he kept a straight face. 'David, David,' he began. 'I know you mean well, but you're just a youth. This Goliath has fought many battles. Frankly, he could eat you for breakfast!' The servants tried not to laugh.

'My lord,' replied David. 'I've killed bears and lions when they threatened my father's sheep. This Goliath will be just like them. God will protect me.'

Saul didn't have a better offer, so he ordered his servants to fit David up with his own armour, the very best. When David finally stood in full armour – helmet, chain mail, sword and shield – he tried to set off, but with the weight of it all he could hardly walk! After struggling for a few moments, he gave up. 'It's no good, my lord. I'm not used to all this.'

And he took it all off and handed it back. Then he took up his wooden staff and his leather sling, and went and chose five smooth round stones from the stream bed nearby. As I watched him walk down into the valley, I felt proud, but I was already wondering how to break the news of his death to our parents.

Our whole army watched, as much in amazement as anything else. A boy with a stick and sling against a human killing machine! Goliath seemed to think the same thing. He laughed at first, as did the Philistine army from the safety of their hill across the valley.

'Am I a dog that you come to me with sticks and stones?' roared Goliath. 'Don't insult me, boy. Go home to your mother while you still can.'

David replied, 'Goliath, despite your fine armour and your weapons, I swear that this day I will feed your flesh to the crows, so all the world will know the God of Israel.'

At this, David fitted one of his five stones to his sling and broke into a run, heading straight towards Goliath, who looked a bit surprised. A moment later David swung his arm and the sling whirred over his head. Goliath barely had time to step forward and raise his spear before the round stone flung from

David's whirring sling hit him squarely in the forehead. It struck with such force that it sank deep into his skull and the giant toppled like a felled tree. I swear we could feel the earth vibrating even up on the hill.

A great cheer broke out among our army. David strode forward, took Goliath's own sword and hacked off the man's huge head. Then he held it up by the hair, dripping blood, first to our army, then to the Philistines. We started to surge down the hill into the valley, and the Philistines started to fall over themselves in their efforts to get away. Goliath's shield carrier was already running for his life.

When we got back from chasing the Philistines, there was a great celebration. And all would have been well if someone hadn't started singing a song about how David was a bigger hero than Saul, which Saul didn't like one bit.

Still, that was all a long time ago. My little brother is King David now – but that's another story!

Name _____

Have you understood the story?

ACTIVITY SHEET 1

1. Why isn't David in the army?

2. Why aren't the two armies fighting at the beginning of the story?

3. Why don't any of the Israelites want to fight Goliath?

4. Why do you think David decides to fight Goliath?

5. Why does King Saul have to make an effort not to laugh at David?

6. What proof does David offer of his ability to fight Goliath?

7. What does David do that shows he is not very strong, or a soldier?

8. What is David good at, apart from fighting?

9. In what way is David's success a good thing for –

   a) the Israelites?
   b) Saul?
   c) his family?
   d) himself?

10. Write a news story for the 'Israelite Echo' newspaper telling the story of David's bravery and achievement. Include:

    • what happened;
    • where and when it happened;
    • who was involved;
    • David's background and why his victory was surprising;
    • what his success meant for his people, his king, his family and himself.

80   RE/Citizenship

PHOTOCOPIABLE

Name _____

Have you understood the story?

ACTIVITY SHEET 2

Circle the right answer.

1. Why isn't David in the army?
   a) He's ill. b) He's scared. c) He's too young.

2. Why aren't the armies fighting at the start of the story?
   a) They're tired out. b) Goliath wants to fight in single combat.
   c) They've made friends.

3. Why don't any of the Israelites want to fight Goliath?
   a) He's huge. b) It's against their religion. c) He's too well armed.

4. Why do you think David decides to fight Goliath?
   a) He wants to show off. b) He doesn't want his God to be insulted.

5. Why does King Saul almost laugh at David?
   a) David looks silly. b) David falls over in the heavy armour.
   c) David seems too young and inexperienced to fight Goliath.

6. What proof does David offer of his ability to fight Goliath?
   a) He has killed a man. b) He can play the harp.
   c) He has killed wild animals.

7. What does David do that shows he is not very strong, or a soldier?
   a) He falls over. b) He takes off the armour because it's too heavy.
   c) He runs away.

8. What is David good at, apart from fighting?
   a) playing the harp b) cricket c) cookery

9. In what way is David's success a good thing for –
   a) the Israelites? (clue: think of the Philistines)
   b) Saul? (clue: kings are proud)
   c) his family? (clue: find the part in the story where David asks,
      'How shall the man who kills him be rewarded?')
   d) himself? (clue: What will people think of David now?)

PHOTOCOPIABLE

RE/Citizenship 81

Local heroes – Native American

TEACHERS' NOTES

> This chapter explores the story 'Monster-slayer and Born-of-water Visit their Father'. It could take up one or more lessons, depending on which activities you choose. The story deals with parenthood and service to the community and could make a good pair with 'The Prodigal Son' (Chapter 3).

Themes

Courage, divine assistance (finding help), parenthood, testing, service to the community

Citizenship scheme of work

- Unit 2 – Choices
- Unit 4 – People who help us
- Unit 7 – Children's rights – human rights

Aims

- To make children consider the idea of courage in the service of the community.

Resources

- The story 'Monster-slayer and Born-of-Water Visit their Father (page 84)
- Copies of the activity sheet on page 86

Background

The Navajo tribe still live in the south-west of the USA, in Arizona. In their religion, mythical figures are regarded as deities. The story of the twin heroes Monster-slayer and Born-of-Water is part of the Navajo story of origin, like the Garden of Eden story in the Old Testament. The twins are the sons of Changing Woman, regarded as the mother of the Navajo, while her husband the Sun is their father. The twins are, in a sense, light and dark aspects of one hero. Service to the community is central to Navajo religion, so it is important that the twins' journey is for this purpose. There is also an element of rite of passage in the story: the boys become men by winning their father's respect.

Whole class starter

❑ Ask the children if they know of any stories in which a hero goes on a journey to find something important or to save somebody. Discuss typical hero stories. In small groups, they could then devise brief hero tale scenarios with the following key elements:

- one or more heroes;
- a major threat to the community, country or world;
- a helper who gives the heroes magical powers;
- a big challenge in which the heroes prove themselves.

❑ Before reading the story 'Monster-slayer and Born-of-water Visit their Father', tell the children that it is a Native American story from the Navajo (pronounced Na-va-hoe) tribe. You could add that it is a tale of twin heroes. As in many Native American stories, it is about heroic deeds performed for the sake of the community.

❑ Now read the story.

82   RE/Citizenship – Ages 9–11

Activities

❏ Ask the children to draw an illustrated map describing events in the story indicating:

- where the brothers set off from;

- where they met Spider Woman;

- the crushing rocks;

- the razor-sharp reeds;

- the ripping cactuses;

- the boiling sands;

- their father's house.

(The story says that this is 'in the west'. This is a good opportunity to teach children the points of the compass.)

❏ They could act out the scene in which the twin heroes meet Spider Woman and receive her help. Mention that this is a typical feature of heroic tales: the hero almost always encounters a helper.

❏ Hand out copies of page 86 and ask the children to use the sheet to plan and write a modern version of the story.

Differentiation

❏ Groups could write the modern versions of the story together, with one person in each group taking responsibility for one section of the story as outlined in the planning sheet.

Extension

❏ The children could find out more about the Navajo on the Internet. There is a large number of sites.

❏ Ask children to think about hero stories they know from films, books and television, and compare them with 'Monster-Slayer and Born-of-Water Visit their Father'. They should find that many have at least some elements in common with this story – and that the true hero is always someone who does something for others.

Plenary session

❏ Ask: 'Is it possible for an ordinary person to be a hero?' What heroic things can the class imagine doing one day, to help their community?

RE/Citizenship – Ages 9–11   83

Monster-Slayer and Born-of-Water Visit their Father

The great mother of the Navajo tribe had twin sons, Monster-Slayer and Born-of-Water. Monsters had been killing the Navajo people and destroying the land, and the twins knew it was up to them to get rid of the monsters. They decided to visit their father, the Sun, to ask him for magical weapons to help them in their task. Although he shined on them every day, they had never met him.

The twins said goodbye to their mother and set off. Soon they saw a thin line of smoke coming out of the ground some way off. They found that this came from an underground house with a sooty ladder disappearing into its smoke hole. They climbed down and found the owner of the house. It was a little, round-bodied grandmother – Spider Woman.

'Welcome, grandchildren,' she said. 'Who are you and where are you from?'

The boys did not answer, so the old woman asked, 'Where are you going?'

'Nowhere special,' they replied. Four times she asked and received the same answer.

Turning to stir some soup she was making, she smiled to herself. 'Perhaps you'd like to visit your father,' she suggested. The twins admitted that this was true, but that they did not know the way to their father's house.

Spider Woman nodded. 'It's a long, dangerous journey,' she said. 'There are monsters along the way, and even when you arrive your father may not be pleased to see you. But if you're sure about this, you should know about the four special dangers: the crushing rocks, the razor-sharp reeds, the ripping cactuses and the boiling sands.'

Spider Woman gave the boys a magic feather charm to protect them and taught them a spell to calm an enemy's anger. They thanked her and set off again.

They came to each of the dangers in turn – the crushing rocks, the razor-sharp reeds, the ripping cactuses and the boiling sands – but overcame each of them with the help of Spider Woman's magic.

Eventually the boys came to their father's house. It stood on the edge of the ocean, where they had seen the sun go down in the west. At the entrance, two huge bears reared up angrily, but the boys calmed them with Spider Woman's spell, and the beasts lay down to sleep. After the bears came a pair of rattlesnakes, who were also sent to sleep by the spell.

84 RE/Citizenship PHOTOCOPIABLE

Then came strong winds and thunderbolts, but even these were changed into a gentle breeze by Spider Woman's charm.

Finally, the boys entered the large, square house. It was built of turquoise stone. At the western end sat a woman. Two handsome young men sat in the south, and two beautiful young women sat opposite them in the north. Seeing the boys, the two young women rose and wrapped them in blankets made from the sky: the rosy sky of dawn, the blue sky of midday, the yellow evening light, and the darkness of night. Then they placed the boys on a shelf, where they lay quietly, waiting to see what would happen next.

Soon the door shook, and in came the Sun. He hung his great golden disc on a peg on the wall, where it shook and clanged for a while before it grew still and silent. Turning angrily, he demanded of the older woman, 'Wife, who were the pair who arrived earlier?' He asked four times before she answered him.

'You've got a nerve!' she replied at last. 'I'm your wife, but these two boys claim to be your sons.' She pointed to the two bundles on the shelf.

Quickly, the Sun grabbed the two boys and threw them at a row of sharp spikes on the wall. Protected by their charms, they just bounced back. He picked them up and threw them at more spikes on each wall of the house, but each time they bounced back.

'What strong boys! How I wish you really were my sons. But since you're not, I'll just boil you to death in here.' Saying, this, he stuffed them into a kind of tent made of branches and skins – a sweat lodge. It was suffocatingly hot in there, but the wind came to the rescue and cooled the boys down.

When they came out unharmed, the Sun put his hands on their shoulders.

'You must be my boys after all,' he announced. 'Come and smoke a pipe with me.' The pipe, however, was poisoned. This time, a caterpillar came to the aid of the boys, placing something in their mouths to protect them from the poison.

'My sons,' said their father at last. 'You have earned my trust. How can I help you?'

'We need magical weapons to save the world,' they said together. 'And only you can provide them.'

'Then you shall have them,' said the Sun.

And so it was that Monster-Slayer and Born-of-Water were able to save their people, and the whole world, from the marauding monsters. Only four of them were allowed to remain: Age, Winter, Poverty and Famine.

Name _____

A tale of heroes

In your story, twin heroes have to go on a journey to save their community.

1. Decide whether your heroes are two boys, two girls, or a boy and a girl.

2. Decide what danger threatens their community.
   A flood? A volcano? A disease? Criminals? A wartime enemy? Something magical?

3. Decide what they need to help them.
   Medicine? Knowledge and advice? Weapons? A map? A magic spell?

4. They meet a helper who gives them important advice. Who is the helper? What does he or she suggest?

5. The twins face four dangers on the way. Decide what they are and how the heroes escape them. Do they follow the helper's advice?

6. The twins meet the person who can give them what they need to save their community. How do they persuade this person to help?

7. How does the story end?

Faith and bravery – Sikhism

TEACHER'S NOTES

> This chapter is designed to be spread over two or three lessons. The story of 'The Five Beloved Ones' could be coupled with 'David and Goliath' (Chapter 12), which is about someone prepared to risk his life for a cause, or 'The Betrayal of Jesus', which also features the theme of trust.

Themes

Bravery, trust, devotion to a cause

Citizenship scheme of work

- Unit 2 – Choices

Aims

- To make children consider the different types of courage needed in modern life. In so doing, they should find out more about themselves and others in the group, reaching an understanding that different people find different things challenging.

Resources

- The story 'The Five Beloved Ones' (page 89)
- Copies of the photocopiable sheet, page 91

Background

Sikhism was founded by Guru Nanak ('Guru' means a special teacher and leader), who was born in 1469. Hence, it was already established by the time of its tenth and final living guru, Guru Gobind Singh. Nonetheless he felt it necessary to form the Khalsa, a group of particularly dedicated men and women prepared to defend their faith. Sikhs believe in the existence of one God and in the importance of service to humanity, truthfulness, tolerance and brotherly love.

Whole class starter

❑ Ask the children what is meant by 'bravery'. Some, especially younger children, may define 'being brave' as not crying when they hurt themselves. Hand out copies of page 91. Looking at the pictures, draw out the idea that bravery may involve overcoming fear (like the climber in the picture), and that bravery can involve trust, either in ourselves or others. Give help where necessary in identifying with the illustrated examples. You could ask, 'What is the girl climber thinking? What does this tell us? Would she be braver if she wasn't afraid? Have you ever made yourself do something you were frightened of?' For the singer having to face an audience, ask 'What's it like performing to an audience? Should we make ourselves do things like that?'

❑ Discuss the following questions:

- Which person do you think is being most brave?
- What different types of bravery can you see?
- Is it possible to feel frightened and still be brave?

❑ Suggest that it is easier to be brave if someone we trust tells us we will be all right. Ask the children to tell the class who they trust, and to think of a time when someone else has helped them to be brave.

❑ Before reading the story, tell the children that it is from the Sikh religion and is set in India in 1699. At this time, the Sikhs had many enemies, including the Emperor of India. Their tenth Guru wanted the Sikhs to defend their faith bravely. At the spring festival of Baisakhi he tested their courage and their faith in God, and in him.

❑ Now read the story.

Activities

❑ Discuss with the children what they think of the five men in the story. Were they brave? Were they right to trust their Guru?

❑ Ask them to imagine they are one of the five men who went into the tent and write about what happened. They could write the story from the point of view of Daya Ram, or one of the other four. Remind the children that:

- They might have been frightened as well as brave.

- They need to say what they think happened in the tent.

- They should say how they felt before and after going into the tent.

They could begin: 'When my beloved Guru asked if anyone would die for God, I felt…'

❑ Ask the children to think about a time when they, or someone they know, was brave. They should draw a picture of the event and write a caption for the picture, explaining how it shows an example of bravery.

❑ Working in groups, the children could compare views on the types of bravery we need in modern daily life. Remind them that people we trust can help us to be brave. The groups should aim to reach an agreement and then work out a presentation of their views to show the class. Children in each group could take turns to explain one kind of bravery while the rest of the group acts a demonstration.

Differentiation

❑ Give children a writing frame for retelling the story:

- 'The Guru showed me into the tent. Quietly, he told me…'

- 'When the Guru gave us our new robes, I felt…'

- 'We came out of the tent and stood by the Guru. The people in the crowd were…'

- 'I'll always remember that day because…'

Extensions

❑ Explore the five 'K's – the things worn by all members of the Khalsa as symbols of their commitment to Sikhism and their readiness to defend it. These are:
Kach Short underpants symbolising the need for speed of movement in defending the faith.
Kara Steel bangle worn on the right wrist as a symbol of the unity of God and of the Sikhs.
Kirpan A sword or dagger, or (for many modern Sikhs) a brooch or medallion in the form of a sword or dagger.
Kesh Long, uncut hair, symbolising submission to the will of God. You could point out that the turban is not a religious requirement, but worn to keep the hair tidy. Sikh boys wear their hair in top-knots before their hair gets long enough to need a turban.
Kangha Comb to keep the hair clean and hold it in place, symbolising cleanliness and self-discipline.
Young Sikhs often join the Khalsa between the ages of 16 and 18, but there is no set age or obligation to join it. The children could consider the concept of symbolism, comparing the five 'K's with the Christian cross. The Sikh taking of amrit could be compared with Christian communion. Both could be compared with secular symbols of commitment to a group, for example an army or cubs uniform.

Plenary session

❑ Ask the children to complete the sentences 'Bravery is…' or 'A brave person is one who…' Attempt to reach a class consensus.

The Five Beloved Ones

'Keep up, Ranjit, or we'll lose you in the crowd.' My mother's voice was anxious. 'We don't want to be looking all over Anandpur for you!'

I hoisted up my sleeping mat and blanket and walked a little faster, scuffing up dust with my sandals. 'Why are there so many people?' I asked my father as I caught up with him. My family are all Sikhs, and I had been to many Sikh meetings before, but none as big as this.

'People come to the spring festival from all over India,' answered my father.

'And there seem to be more of us each year.'

'Yes,' added my mother. 'But I think this year will be special. I've heard that our leader, Guru Gobind Singh, has something to tell us.'

I sensed her excitement and wondered what the Guru had to say. It seemed that others were wondering the same thing. Even my little sister Ritu held my father's hand more tightly than usual.

The crowd surged through the town of Anandpur, growing like a river in flood. Soon, we were slowing down, as we approached the meeting place. We were near the front of the crowd, on a slope facing downhill. As people sat down, I was able to see a large tent below us. The morning sun lit up a sea of turbans and headscarves, of many colours. From here and there came the sound of music. I could smell sweet incense on the air.

After prayers, an expectant hush fell on the crowd. We could all tell something important was about to happen. Sure enough, out of the tent below emerged a handsome bearded man in a military uniform.

'It's Guru Gobind Singh,' whispered my mother. I stood up for a better view.

Holding a shining sword high in the air, the Guru spoke. His voice carried loud and clear across the silent crowd. 'Which of you is prepared to die?' he demanded. There was a shocked silence. 'Who is ready to die, for God and for Sikhism?' A murmur ran through the crowd. 'Which of you will offer his head for the sake of his faith?'

Some people now looked worried. A few were even starting to leave. They must have thought their beloved leader had gone mad! Finally, I could see a disturbance in the crowd below. A man was pushing his way through. I later learned that this man was called Daya Ram.

'I am prepared to give up my life for God and for my faith,' announced Daya Ram in a firm voice.

Some of those who had started to leave now waited to see what would happen next. The crowd was on its feet. I pulled at my father's sleeve and he lifted me up onto his shoulders. Ritu was already in my mother's arms. From my vantage point, I saw the Guru lead Daya Ram into his tent. The sound of a sword slicing the air cut through the silence of the crowd, immediately followed by the thud of something heavy hitting the ground. A moment later, Guru Gobind Singh reappeared. He held up his sword. It now dripped with something dark and red – blood! I gasped. Ritu whimpered. My mother clung to my father's arm.

'Who else has a faith so strong that he is ready to die for God?' asked the Guru of the crowd. To my amazement, another man pushed his way out of the crowd and declared himself ready to die. Like the first, he disappeared into the tent with Guru Gobind Singh. Again there came the sound of a sword swiftly parting the air and the thud of something heavy hitting the ground. I expected to see a head roll out of the tent! Instead, out came the Guru, his sword even bloodier than before.

Three more times this happened. By the time the fifth man had offered his life for God, the Guru's smart uniform was splattered with blood. Many people in the crowd had hurried away. I wondered how many more brave men would die in the same way. But then, an even more incredible thing happened. The Guru stepped smiling out of his tent, but this time he was followed by all five of the men who had offered their lives to God. We had thought they were dead, but here they were, alive and well, and dressed in bright golden robes and turbans, with blue sashes round their waists. Each held up a shining sword.

'How…?' I started to ask my father, before being shushed into silence.

The Guru stepped forward. 'These men have proved their courage and their faith,' he said. 'Each was prepared to die for their faith in God. For this, they will be called the Panj Pyare – the Five Beloved Ones. They are now my brothers. They are the first members of the Khalsa, a special group of Sikhs who will be responsible for defending the Sikh faith against its enemies. Any Sikh who is brave, pure-hearted and devoted to Sikhism may join the Khalsa – rich or poor, man or woman.'

Guru Gobind Singh then prepared a welcome ceremony for the five men. He made a drink of water and sugar, called amrit, and sprinkled a little over them and gave them some to drink. The Guru and his wife also drank amrit. By the end of that day, most of the people at that huge meeting had taken part in this ceremony, including my parents.

Name _____

Being brave

CHAPTER 14

How we treat others – Sikhism

TEACHERS' NOTES

> The chapter is based on the story of 'Guru Gobind Singh and the Donkey' and is, in part, about how we treat others. It could be coupled with the Buddhist story, 'The King's Elephant' (Chapter 2), which teaches that we may treat others badly through following a bad example. The section is designed to be spread over two or three sessions.

Themes

Appearances, how people treat us, kindness to animals

Citizenship scheme of work

- Unit 1 – Taking part
- Unit 3 – Animals and us
- Unit 5 – Living in a diverse world

Aims

To encourage children to consider:
- how they treat other people, and animals;
- how the way they present themselves influences how they are treated;
- how people reach group decisions.

Resources

- The story 'Gobind Singh and the Donkey (page 94)
- Copies of the photocopiable sheets on pages 96 and 97

Background

The Sikh belief in tolerance and humanity is shown in the story 'Guru Gobind Singh and the Donkey' by his kindness towards the donkey and his patient teaching of the villagers. For more on Guru Gobind Singh and Sikhism, see Chapter 13, 'Background'.

Whole class starter

❑ Ask the following questions:

- What does it mean to 'treat someone well'? Ask for examples.
- What does it mean to 'treat someone badly'? Ask for examples.
- Should we treat everyone equally? Or should we, for example, be kinder to friends and family?
- How important is it to treat animals kindly? Should we be equally kind to chimpanzees, dogs, frogs and stick insects?

❑ Hand out copies of page 96 and ask the class to talk about how people are treating others in the pictures. They could write a brief comment on each picture.

❑ Before reading the story 'Guru Gobind Singh and the Donkey', tell children that it is from the Sikh religion and is about Guru Gobind Singh, the first great teacher of that religion. If you have already read 'The Five Beloved Ones' (Chapter 13) with the class, tell them this is about the same guru and is set at the same time (around 1700) in India.

❑ Now read the story.

Activities

❑ Working individually or in pairs, the children should imagine that they are the donkey in the story. They have to write a diary entry for one typical day in the life of the donkey.

92 RE/Citizenship – Ages 9–11

- In small groups, the children could take it in turns to act out a new child joining their class, choosing one of the following lines. They must make their voice and the way they move suit the line. They can use their own name or make one up.

  - 'Hi, everybody. My name's _____. I'm new here, I live over the road. So, what are you all doing, then?'

  - 'Um… er… excuse me – I'm not sure if I should be here. Sorry to be a nuisance but I'm lost. Oh, my name's _____ by the way.'

  - 'Right, weeds! My name's _____ I'm new around here, but let's get one thing straight – I don't take any stick from anyone. Right? Give me one of your toffees!'

  Ask the children to discuss how they would treat each of these newcomers, and how they think other people are likely to treat them.

- Remind the children of the scene in the story where the townspeople hold a meeting and decide what to do about the tiger. Split the class into groups of four or five and give each group a copy of the activity sheet on page 97. Read through the scenario with them and then ask them to come up with a plan based on the prompts on the sheet.

Differentiation

- You could make the first activity easier by giving the children the following sentence starters as a framework:
  - 'At dawn today I…'
  - 'My master said to me… and gave me a…'
  - 'Most of the day I had to…'
  - 'I really wish that …'

- As a more challenging alternative to the donkey diary, or as an activity for fast finishers, the children could write the donkey's diary entry for the day featured in the story, paying close attention to what actually happens. A possible sentence starter framework is:

  - 'Today was amazing! A kind-looking man led me…'

  - 'Then he laid something on my back…'

  - 'When people saw me coming, they…'

  - 'I ran into the forest to escape. I felt so…'

  - 'Finally…'

Extension

- The children could design a poster to encourage kindness to donkeys or other animals. You could give them leaflets or posters from groups such as IFAW or the RSPCA to use as a model.

- The children could devise and perform a play using one or more of the 'newcomers'. The play could begin with the lines given and go on to explore the responses of others.

- The children could write a story in which some people misjudge a situation, like the townspeople in the story. For example, they might all get the wrong idea about a newcomer and treat this person in a way that the person does not deserve.

Plenary session

- As a class, try to agree on how to complete these sentences:

  - 'We should treat other people…'

  - 'If we want to be treated well by other people, we should…'

  - 'Animals deserve…'

  - 'The best way to make a group decision is to…'

RE/Citizenship – Ages 9–11 93

Gobind Singh and the Donkey

Guru Gobind Singh was strolling through the town one day. Since it was the hottest part of the day, many people were indoors and it was quiet, apart from the buzzing of flies. But the quiet was suddenly broken by a long, loud noise – a cross between somebody wailing and a water pump in urgent need of oiling. The Guru looked round. It was a tired old donkey which belonged to a man who sold vegetables in the town market. The poor animal's back seemed to be bent into a sinking curve by all the sacks of vegetables it carried every day. Its coarse grey coat was worn thin where the sacks usually sat. The creature complained bitterly to the world with its noisy braying.

The Guru knew this animal. It was mocked and teased by people all day as it carried its burdens: 'You stupid donkey!' they would shout after it. Only a few children felt sorry for the donkey – along with the kind hearted Guru. 'My friend,' he said to the braying donkey, 'if that was the roar of a tiger, people wouldn't laugh at you!'

The Guru thought for a moment. At home he had a tiger skin, a present from a friend. So he took the donkey by its halter and led it to his home on the edge of the town. In his peaceful garden he fed the hungry animal beans and carrots and filled a trough with fresh cool water for it to drink. While it was eating, the Guru went indoors and fetched the tiger skin. It had belonged to a huge tiger, and it easily disguised the puzzled donkey when the Guru gently laid it on the animal's back. The tiger's fierce, roaring jaws fitted neatly over the donkey's long ears, hiding them from view.

When the donkey had eaten and drunk its fill, the Guru led it back into the town centre. Near the market place he set it free. Knowing its way home, the donkey plodded on, quietly enjoying the taste of beans and carrots lingering on its tongue. But people seemed to be behaving very oddly today. Instead of offering insults, slaps and teasing, they hastily moved out of the donkey's way, with looks of fear and horror on their faces. He couldn't understand it at all. It was the centre of the market at midday, and yet the place rapidly became deserted. Even the donkey's owner fled on seeing him. Sparing only a few moments to reflect on this, the donkey ambled over to his master's vegetable stall. No one was nearby to hit him or shout at him, so he happily feasted. All the fresh fruit and vegetables he could eat!

Meanwhile, the people who lived in the town hastily gathered for a meeting. The self appointed chairman, the vegetable stall holder, stood on a box to address the crowd.

'Something must be done immediately about this danger. We cannot allow tigers to roam the streets of the town. None of us will be safe, and people will go elsewhere to buy their fruit and vegetables.'

'We could pray,' suggested an old woman.

'We could leave goat's meat out for the tiger so that it wasn't hungry enough to eat us,' suggested the town butcher.

Then the Guru spoke. 'I have a suggestion. Why don't we make a lot of noise with drums, and cooking pots, and shouting, and frighten it out of the town back into the jungle?'

The meeting took a vote and it was agreed to follow the Guru's suggestion. Everyone went home and found whatever they could that would make a lot of noise. All over town, old cooking pots and ladles, trays and sticks, drums, bells and rattles quickly appeared.

Under the Guru's direction, the people approached the market, making as much noise as they could. Although afraid at first, they found that the shouting and banging helped to give them courage. The donkey, however, was bewildered and distressed. What was going on? This was worse than being taunted. He fled before the crowd, who were encouraged by the flight of this fierce tiger from their mighty cooking pots and drums.

Many of the people felt brave for the first time they could remember, so when the donkey-tiger entered the forest they continued their pursuit. But when the exhausted and terrified donkey let loose a desperate braying that echoed all around the forest, the people were stopped in their tracks. A braying tiger? Surely, this was just the market donkey. And sure enough, as they stopped their noise and drew close, the tiger skin snagged on a low branch and came off. There stood the donkey!

The Guru quietly told the people to keep back. He went and patted and soothed the frightened animal and led it back to its owner. 'Learn a lesson from this, all of you,' he said to the crowd. 'Here stands a poor old animal. He wore the skin of a tiger but he had the heart of a donkey!'

Name _____

How we treat others

ACTIVITY SHEET 1

....
....
....

....
....
....

RE/Citizenship — PHOTOCOPIABLE

Making a plan

You and your class are trapped inside your school. Your teacher is missing. Outside it is snowing. It is snowing so hard that nobody can come to school and rescue you. Hungry tigers have escaped from the zoo and are prowling in the school yard: they know where you are and they are trying to find a way into the school. Mobile phones don't work. You have no food supplies – everyone ate their packed lunches hours ago.

1. What could you do to get out?

2. How will you decide what to do? You could appoint a leader, take a vote or keep talking about it till everyone agrees (but don't forget the tigers are getting closer all the time…)

3. Decide what you are going to do.

4. Explain your decision to the rest of the class.

PHOTOCOPIABLE

Everyone's different – Sufism

TEACHERS' NOTES

This chapter, based on the Sufi story 'The Shopkeeper and the Parrot', could be tackled in a single lesson or spread over two, depending on which activities you choose. It could be told alongside 'The Five Beloved Ones' (Chapter 13) or 'Gobind Singh and the Donkey' (Chapter 14) – both of which look at appearances.

Themes
Appearances, gratitude, cause and effect, how we treat animals

Citizenship scheme of work
- Unit 1 – Taking part
- Unit 3 – Animals and us
- Unit 5 – Living in a diverse world
- Unit 9 – Respect for property

Aims
- To make children consider the fact that all people are unique and that therefore we cannot entirely judge one person by another.
- To make children think about how we treat animals.

Resources
- The story 'The Shopkeeper and the Parrot' (page 100)
- Copies of the photocopiable activity sheet on page 103

Whole class starter
❑ Put the class into groups of three or four. Using copies of page 103 as a prompt, the children should discuss the ways in which they are different from other children in the group and the ways in which they are similar. They could then collaborate in drawing a large diagram to show these similarities and differences. The diagram could show a face for each child in the group with lines between them, and the similarities and differences written along the lines. The children could also use colour coding – for example, writing in green for similarities and red for differences. Explain that this will be used later when they look at how school could be changed to work better with the differences between the children.

❑ Before reading the story 'The Shopkeeper and the Parrot', tell the children that it is a Sufi story. Explain that Sufism is a religion that developed from Islam. Many Sufi stories have a 'moral': they are designed to teach a lesson.

❑ Now read the story.

Activities
❑ Ask the children the following questions to check how well they have understood the story. Note that the questions get much more difficult towards the end.

- What is special about Sweet Tongue?
- Why does the shopkeeper buy him?

Background
Sufism is the mystical branch of Islam. Its followers believe it is the spiritual path to a mystical union with God. Its followers may isolate themselves from society or, more usually, join a Sufi order. The movement seems to have begun in the late 7th century as a reaction against the strict formality of orthodox teaching but is deeply rooted in Islamic spiritualism.

- Why does the shopkeeper's business improve after he buys Sweet Tongue?

- Why does the shopkeeper hit him?

- How does the shopkeeper try to cure Sweet Tongue?

- How does Sweet Tongue misunderstand the dervish's appearance?

- What lesson does the shopkeeper learn from the dervish?

❑ Give the children the following task: 'Imagine you are an RSPCA officer. You visit the shopkeeper's shop after a tip off from a customer that a parrot has been mistreated. First write a dialogue between the shopkeeper and the RSPCA officer. Then write the RSPCA officer's report on the incident, including your opinion as to whether or not the shopkeeper should be prosecuted for cruelty.' In a follow up session children could act out the dialogues.

❑ Drawing on the starter activity and the dervish's lesson, ask children to write an essay on how schools could best allow for the differences between people.

- Should all children have to do the same lessons? For example, should a child who is very good at maths do more maths, or less maths, than others?

- Should the rules be the same for all? For example, should a child who finds it difficult to sit still be allowed to wander about?

- Should children be encouraged to be different? If so, how?

If you asked the children to make diagrams showing their similarities and differences, use these as a starting point for this activity.

Differentiation

❑ For the RSPCA officer task you could offer the children opening lines:
RSPCA officer: It has been reported to me that a parrot has been cruelly mistreated in this shop. I can see that this parrot is bald. How did that happen?
Shopkeeper: Believe me, I didn't mean to be cruel…

Extension

❑ Children could use the Internet to find more Sufi stories, read them and comment on what lesson they teach.

❑ They could also research the work of the RSPCA.

Plenary session

❑ Ask the children, 'What do the dervish's words teach us about people, and about how people appear to be?'

The Shopkeeper and the Parrot

A shopkeeper was in the market one day when he saw a beautiful parrot for sale. The bright colours of its feathers filled him with joy. He asked the owner, 'How much for that parrot?' As was the custom, they bartered. The owner named a ridiculously high price; the shopkeeper shrugged and said he would offer only a fraction of this sum. Then the owner lowered his price a little, and the would-be buyer raised his just enough to show that he was still interested. This went on for several minutes, until they agreed on a price and the shopkeeper, trying to hide his delight, became the proud owner of the parrot.

The shopkeeper hurried back to his shop and found the perfect place to hang the parrot's cage, where it would attract customers from outside. His shop had not been doing well lately. But his wonderful new parrot would change all that!

As the man soon found out, this was no ordinary parrot. Like many parrots, it could speak. Most parrots, however, can only copy the phrases they hear – 'Who's a pretty boy then?' and that sort of thing – with little or no understanding of what they are saying. This parrot, on other hand, seemed to understand the words it spoke, and soon began to delight the shopkeeper's customers by having conversations with them.

'You're more than a parrot,' said the shopkeeper. 'You're my friend and business partner. I will call you Sweet Tongue.'

The shopkeeper's business was soon doing so well, with all the interest aroused by his parrot, that he was able to start selling a new line of medicines. A month or so later, he invested in a wide range of healing oils, ointments, potions and tonics.

Business continued to grow. He was well on the way to becoming a wealthy man. And he still enjoyed his chats with Sweet Tongue in the moments between customers and when the shop closed at the end of the day. They became such friends that the man decided to reward Sweet Tongue with the freedom of the shop. No longer caged, the happy parrot flew around the shop, displaying his plumage to the customers in its full magnificence.

One sad morning, though, the shopkeeper opened up his shop to find all his bottles of lotions and potions broken and spilled on the floor. Sweet Tongue had been flying around in the night and knocked them off the shelves. The poor man clutched his head and wrung his hands. All the money he had invested in his new goods was trickling across the messy floor and under his doorway onto the street!

In anger, the man caught hold of Sweet Tongue. 'You wretched bird!' he cried. 'I'll pull your feathers out!' But instead he banged the poor bird's head on the counter several times, so hard that the bird was stunned. Then he threw the limp bird into its cage and began, sorrowfully, to clear up the mess.

For weeks, the shopkeeper's profits were almost non-existent. He worked hard to replace his stock, little by little, but it was slow going. Worse, Sweet Tongue seemed to have been permanently injured by the blows to his head. He had lost all his head feathers and was now bald. Worst of all, the parrot had lost his powers of speech. He sat silently moping in his cage. He was no longer a delight to the customers and business went from bad to worse.

The shopkeeper tried one thing after another to restore his parrot's broken health. He rubbed oils into his bald head, without effect. He fed tasty nuts and seeds to the bird. He hired a musician to play his flute to Sweet Tongue. He even managed to buy a female parrot and placed her cage in front of Sweet Tongue's cage. Pleading with his old friend, the man promised to set them both free to fly around the shop if only he would speak again.

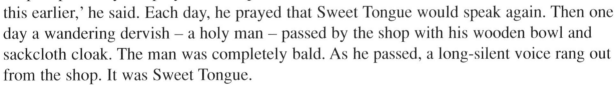

None of this worked. In the end there was nothing for the shopkeeper to try but prayer. 'Perhaps I should have tried this earlier,' he said. Each day, he prayed that Sweet Tongue would speak again. Then one day a wandering dervish – a holy man – passed by the shop with his wooden bowl and sackcloth cloak. The man was completely bald. As he passed, a long-silent voice rang out from the shop. It was Sweet Tongue.

'Hey – how did you end up bald? Did you break a few potion bottles like me?'

The shopkeeper was overjoyed. His parrot had spoken at last! He invited the dervish in and told him the story of Sweet Tongue and his lost powers. The dervish went up to Sweet Tongue's cage.

'So, you think you and I are bald for the same reasons?'

'Naturally,' answered Sweet Tongue. 'Why else?'

The dervish smiled. 'My friend. Let me teach you something. No two leaves on a tree are the same. Nor are any two people, or two creatures, the same. Some think about life and some do not. Some are wise and some are not. Nothing causes more trouble than the human habit of judging things by appearances. Take bees, for example: some make sweet honey, while others will only sting you.'

The dervish was silent and looked hard at the shopkeeper. In a moment, the shopkeeper realised that he had been taught a lesson. He rushed after the dervish, but the man had disappeared. What's more, no one else had noticed a bald dervish in the town that day.

As for Sweet Tongue, he remained bald. He continued to speak, but not as often as before. And the customers were often mystified by his words.

How are you different?

Use these questions to find out how you are similar to, or different from, other children in your group. Ignore your appearance, your age and whether you are a boy or girl.

1. Do you like to be the centre of attention? *(For example, having people laugh at your jokes or listening to you telling stories.)*

2. Would you be happy spending two hours on your own at home?

3. Do you like to be the first person to try something difficult, like jumping over a stream or giving the answer to a new kind of sum in class? Or would you rather wait until someone else has done it first?

4. Which of these sentences is more true of you?
   a) I like meeting new people and making new friends.
   b) I don't make new friends easily, so I prefer to stick with people I know.

5. What do you like doing? *for example: reading, drawing, playing football, chatting to friends, playing computer games*

6. Which of these sentences is most true of you?
   a) I think bullies should be severely punished.
   b) I think bullies are unhappy. We should try to understand them.
   c) I think if people are bullied it's their own fault.

7. How important do you think honesty is? Is it all right to tell 'fibs' to get out of trouble?

8. Are you an animal lover? Do you think we should always be kind to animals?

PHOTOCOPIABLE

RE/Citizenship 103

Useful websites

Citizenship
www.standards.dfes.gov.uk/schemes2/ks1-2citizenship
Gives full details on Citizenship units at Key Stages 1 and 2.

All religions
www.bbc.co.uk/religion/religions

Extremely informative and well organised site giving details of history, customs, beliefs, worship, holy days and features of fourteen different religions (including atheism).

www.ers.north-ayrshire.gov.uk/topics.htm
This page gives links to all the North Ayrshire topics pages, including pages of links to resources on each of the major religions. Each page is divided up into General, Festivals, Stories, Traditions and Resources (books). These are all subdivided into pages suitable for either pupils or teachers/parents. Asterisks indicate interactive pages.

www.teachingreligion.com/index.html
Useful US website providing information on many religions to school teachers. It also discusses issues of teaching religion and offers classroom activities.

Buddhism
www.dharmaforkids.com

A user-friendly site with well organised information on many aspects of Buddhism. Includes stories from the Buddha's life, art gallery, activities, teachers' notes and an interactive nun (click on her image on the home page to see more).

www.fwbo.org
The official site of the Friends of the Western Buddhist Order. Not aimed at children, but clear and well organised.

Christianity
www.request.org.uk

Well designed and balanced site with sections for infants, KS2 and above, and teachers (including a 'Teacher's Guide to Using the Internet in Religious Education').

www.topmarks.co.uk/religious/default.aspx

Illustrated interactive versions of the stories of the birth of Jesus and Easter (also Moses and Joseph).

Hinduism
www.btinternet.com/~vivekananda/schools1.htm

A helpful and informative site on many aspects of Hinduism. The 'Key Stage 1' pages appear to be for all primary (but more suitable for KS2); the 'Key Stage 2 and 3' pages are actually for secondary. The links page has links to stories and to a site featuring 'virtual poojas' – Hindu worship in interactive cyber form (www.eprarthana.com/virtual/vpooja.asp). Choose your Hindu god. Best with speakers on in order to hear the mantras.

www.hindu.org
Comprehensive site with section for teachers.

Islam
www.islam-guide.com/contents-wide.htm

Information on Islam from a believer's viewpoint. Presents a scientific case for the truth of the Qu'ran.

Jainism
www.jainworld.com/index.asp

Very comprehensive site giving information on Jainism: history, philosophy, educational materials. The 'Educational materials' section contains a sub-section with 32 Jain stories, including a version of 'King Hansa'.

The literature section includes
www.jainworld.org/general/prem/Cartoons/cartoon.htm

which tells the story of Bhagwan Rishabhdev in comic format.

Judaism
www.twocandles.com

Jewish songs for and by children.

www.topmarks.co.uk/religious/default.aspx
Illustrated interactive versions of the stories of Moses and Joseph (also Jesus and Easter). Moses story links to a good page on the Ten Commandments, with an activity page.

Native American (Navajo)
http://navajo-indian.org

Starting point for information on all aspects of Navajo life.

www.bedtime-story.com/bedtime-story/navajo-rainbow.htm
Child friendly version of the birth story of the twins Monster-Slayer and Born-of-Water.

www.ewebtribe.com/NACulture/stories.htm
Links to Native American legends and stories.

Sikhism
www.sikhnet.com

An interesting and wide-ranging site primarily aimed at Sikhs but of interest to anyone who wants to find out about this religion. The 'SikhiWiki' is an encyclopedia of Sikhism, including an excellent introduction to the religion. The 'Sikh Youth' section contains a collection of illustrated stories (www.sikhnet.com/s/SikhStories). The Gurbani section (www.sikhnet.com/Gurbani) has a large selection of audio files of music and stories. (You will need Real Player to listen.)

Sufism
www.windsofchange.net/archives/cat_features_sufi_wisdom.php

Sufi wisdom and deceptively simple stories that children will probably be able to read but which they will need to think about.

www.zahuri.org/Sufistories.html
Short Sufi stories, not especially aimed at children but short enough for them to read or for you to adapt.